The Black Presence

James Walvin

The Black Presence

A documentary history of the Negro in England, 1555-1860

Schocken Books • New York

Published in U.S.A. in 1972
by Schocken Books Inc.
67 Park Avenue, New York, N.Y. 10016

© 1971 by James Walvin

Library of Congress Catalog Card No. 75–169829

Printed in Great Britain

Contents

Acknowledgements

Without the hospitality of a variety of friends the research for this book would have proved impossible. Over the years their homes (particularly those of the Beezer, Bridge and Clarke families) have been freely opened to me and I thank them for their unfailing perseverance with a demanding guest. To Gerald Aylmer and Barrie Dobson I owe sincere thanks for the friendly tolerance towards, and connivance at, my periodic and sudden disappearances from my place of work. Of the many libraries used, the Goldsmith's Library and the Institute of Jamaica have provided me with the greatest help and consideration. Lt-Col. Lloyd-Baker allowed me to consult the Granville Sharp papers and in so doing greatly helped with his friendly advice. Colleagues and students at the Universities of York and the West Indies and at Waterloo and McMaster Universities in Canada, have helped with their fertile and constructive criticisms. Over the past three years Michael Craton has striven to make me say and write precisely what I mean. For this, and many other kindnesses I thank him. Finally, but above all others, to my friend and constant teacher, Gwyn Williams, I owe more than he would care to know.

JAMES WALVIN

University of York
March 1971

To
Rosie and Selena
Who told me both sides
of the Jamaican story

Preface

The history of the black community in Britain can be traced to the mid-sixteenth century and clearly predates the rise of modern racialism. But the white reaction to Africans from this early date contains most of the ingredients which were to appear in the racialist thought of the late nineteenth and twentieth centuries. To a large extent certain fears, about employment, black immigration and miscegenation, are common throughout. Racialism is thus not solely a product of modern capitalist society. There is a legacy of English racial attitudes towards the Negro, the roots of which go deep into the age of European expansion in the sixteenth and seventeenth centuries and find their origins in misunderstandings, fears and commercial exploitation.

A full and convincing examination of the history of the black community and of English racial attitudes has never been published. Original primary material tends to be fragmented and dispersed while historical analyses have so far been detailed but limited in scope, and do not illustrate the continuity of the relationship between the Negro and English society. The material in the present volume is offered as a first step in this direction. The content of the book follows the pattern of the English involvement in slave trading: its origins, growth, collapse and immediate aftermath.

Introduction

"We must agree with those who have declared that the public good of this kingdom requires that some restraint should be laid on the unnatural increase of *blacks* imported into it."[1] With these words Edward Long, a vituperative Jamaican planter, pointed bitterly to a much discussed 'social problem' in London in 1772. By this time, the late eighteenth century, the economic well-being of Britain was closely bound up with the prosperity brought by the trade with Africa and the New World. Any understanding of the African trade, a trade which altered the face of three continents, Europe, Africa and the Americas, must begin with a glance at its size and scope.

Spices, tusks and gold, among the first African attractions, were swiftly rendered economically insignificant by the expanding labour demands of the New World colonies. Those traders already experienced in West Africa were aware of the strategic and personal vulnerability of the Africans. The Spaniards and Portuguese had already begun to reap the fruits of African discord by pitching African against African. It was however to be the British in the eighteenth century, with their unrivalled maritime power, their expansive colonial markets and their buoyant domestic economy, who were to perfect the details and the mechanics of the slave trade. Over a period of four hundred years between eight and ten and a half million Africans were imported into the New World.[2] Between the European rediscovery of the Americas and the American War of Independence many more Africans than white Europeans were settled in the New World. The African was the pioneer of American settlement before the nineteenth century.

By the mid-eighteenth century, at the height of the plantation society's prosperity, British ships were ferrying annually
tens of thousands of Africans into bondage and returning to
England with the produce of the New World. Contributing
perhaps as much as one-third to Britain's total economic
development the triangular trade between Britain, West
Africa and the West Indies underpinned Britain's transition
towards an industrial society.[3] When John Hawkins sold his
first batch of Africans into slavery in 1563, no one envisaged
the dimensions to which the trade would grow and the global
importance it would assume. The first major British involvement in the slave trade was *ad hoc* and haphazard. As with all
areas of maritime trade, there were enormous risks and an
inherent incalculability. These remained throughout the
history of the slave trade. Disease among slaves could wipe out
the profits for a whole trip. The slave forts might be empty on
arrival. The risks increased with the constant warfare of the
eighteenth century. Hurricanes in the West Indies added to
the normal maritime delays from storms and were a further
expense to the enterprise. Insurance rates, for example,
customarily doubled for voyages to the West Indies during the
hurricane season, a time which coincided with the harvesting
of the sugar crop. But, despite all these problems, the potential
for profit outweighed the prospects of losses in the minds of the
British investors, slave merchants, planters, insurance under-
writers and bankers.

"There is nothing which contributes more to the development of the colonies and the cultivation of their soil than the
laborious toil of the Negroes."[4] With these words a decree of
Louis XIV in 1670 pin-pointed precisely the causal connection
between the growth of the plantation colonies and the rise of
the slave trade. The triangular trade began with an occasional
foray into the West Indies and South America with black
labour for the early Spanish and Portuguese colonies, but in the
seventeenth century it was the development of the British and
French West Indian islands which produced the massive
expansion in slave trading. By the time of the Restoration of
Charles II the African had become the life-blood of the West

Indies and the supply of enslaved black labour was placed on an organised, that is monopoly, footing in order to satisfy the labour demands of the colonies. This dependence upon African labour was by no means total, or apparent, until the introduction throughout the islands by the mid-seventeenth century of labour intensive monoculture crops, particularly sugar. Early explorations and settlement of the islands had been undertaken by Europeans, Indians and relatively small numbers of Africans, but the growth of the sugar economies demanded massive infusions of cheap, malleable slave labour. Africa seemed to offer a supply of labour that was inexhaustible and cheap, while the goods exchanged in return for the Africans gave an added fillip to domestic industry. Within the space of a century the prospects afforded by the African trade fundamentally revised the framework of British economic expansion. Elizabeth I may have had reservations about the morality of British involvement in the early slave missions but a century later the Court of Charles II, relegating morality behind expansion, actively invested in and patronised the slave trade.[5]

By the early eighteenth century plantations in the West Indies were expanding on the labour of their black slaves. Dependence on African slaves had taken on addictive proportions. The demand for healthy males resulted in sexual imbalance and a relatively low number of slave births and conditions in the West Indies and on the Middle Passage led to a high death rate. Prices of slaves therefore increased considerably throughout the century. The economic system which evolved had begun to over-reach itself even at the point when, to contemporaries, West Indian prosperity seemed at a peak. Crudely put, the plantation system contained within itself the causes of its own downfall. The institution of slavery entailed not merely the dehumanisation and brutalisation of generations of Africans but also involved the economic imprisonment and debasement of the planters themselves.

In the seventeenth and eighteenth century there was never any doubt in the minds of engaged contemporaries about the central importance of the African, both to the West Indies and, directly and indirectly, to Britain. To purchase the African, manufactures poured into Africa; the African's labour tapped the resources of the Americas. The African, by universal agreement, was the flexed muscle of the British empire. Produce and profits from the West Indies flowed into Britain while the needs of the plantation economies were met with British manufactures. Through the African trade fishing villages blossomed into international ports. The whole web of the triangular trade was held together by British maritime strength backed up by the invisible commercial sinews of British banking and insurance. Located at the heart of this commerce was the enslaved African, whose central economic role, conceded by contemporaries, has been confirmed by historical analysis.

It was one thing to concede the economic importance of the African; it was quite another to justify the treatment to which he was subjected and yet the relevant literature tried constantly to fulfil both tasks. When vested interest groups sought to describe the relationship between British prosperity and the enslaved African they invariably embarked on long, convoluted, conscience-stricken justifications for the treatment meted out to the slaves. Whenever varied interest groups sought to advance their own claims to a share in the Africa trade they generally presented their case not as a simple economic proposition, but as a moral enterprise, justifiable on the grounds of an alleged inferiority of the Negro. The distinctive qualities of the African, noted in the sixteenth century, became the hallmarks of inferiority by the eighteenth. Even by the late sixteenth century British commercial practice, and the legislation defending that commerce, was actively treating the African as a form of subhuman; a species of property, or a simple commodity. Alongside this commercial *fait accompli* thrived a multitude of tracts, pamphlets, handbills and books whose purpose was to defend and justify that commerce. Concerned essentially with encouraging and continuing slavery and the slave trade this outpouring of popular literature succeeded in hiding its crude purpose behind a theoretical façade based upon the 'nature' of the African, his uniqueness and indispensability. The slave lobby's philosophy took on the form of an ideology whose theoretical justification was complex and eclectic, a confused patchwork of evidence culled from anthropological, biblical and economic sources.

In defending the involvement with slavery the slave lobby did not rest content with a simple presentation of the economic facts. For instance, when defending the monopoly of the Royal African Company stress was frequently placed on the reasons for enslaving the African. It was claimed that slavery was an improvement for the heathen African, offering him the superior physical conditions of life on the plantations and the blessings of Christianity. Africans alone, others claimed, were able to endure plantation work since they were accustomed to similar geo-physical conditions in West Africa. Others maintained that slavery saved thousands of African prisoners of war from a brutal death at the hands of their African captors, conveniently ignoring the degree to which African warfare was stimulated by the European slave-trading presence.[6]

With the increasing involvement in Africa printed accounts of African life had grown in numbers and in popularity. Sailors, merchants, doctors and scientists collected a wide variety of anthropological data on West African life. Drawing selectively upon this corpus of apparently accurate first-hand information the defenders of slavery offered their readers descriptions of the African which were designed to place him beyond the pale of British comprehension and sympathy, transforming him into a crude caricature and a fitting object for commercial rape. All the evidence pointed to the African's difference; in the hands of the slave lobby this was used to prove his inequality and to justify the continuing existence of African slavery.

When the paper war between the supporters and opponents of slavery reached a crescendo of bitterness towards the end of the eighteenth century the slave lobby fell back increasingly upon the economic necessity of slavery. They calculated that every slave in the West Indies gave employment to no fewer than six workers in Britain. "To those who contend that this commerce should be reprobated as entirely repugnant to moral laws and the gospel, this answer might perhaps be given—that there are, and necessarily must be, many institutions, considering the depravity of human nature, and the state of society in general, equally incompatible with morality and Christianity."[7] Few writers were as honest as this, most preferring to present their justification of the African trade in terms of the African's alleged inferiority. The slave lobby offered the reading public a stereotyped African in an attempt to blunt the all-too-obvious edges of that lobby's inhumanity. Once the African was divested of his humanity, his role within the imperial economic framework seemed clear and comprehensible.

The alarm expressed in England at the large numbers of Negroes settling in London in the last quarter of the eighteenth century gave strength to the slave-owners' case. "The practice of importing Negro servants into these kingdoms is said to be already a grievance that requires a remedy and yet it is every-day encouraged, insomuch that the number in this metropolis only is supposed to be near 20,000."[8] As the century advanced black immigration increased, as did the concern of startled white observers.[9] The immediate cause of black immigration was the expansion of the triangular trade and the return of absentee planters with their retinue of black retainers, a move-ment of population which also troubled the French.[10] Few contemporaries knew, apparently, that London's black com-munity was first seen in the reign of Elizabeth I.

In 1596 Elizabeth sent a letter to the Lord Mayor of London and other cities saying that according to "Her Majesty's under-standing . . . there are of late divers blackamoores brought into these realms, of which kind there are already here to manie, considerynge how God had blessed this land with great increase of people . . ."[11] In July of that year the monarch again expressed her views about black settlers, asserting ". . . that those kinde of people may be well spared in this realme, being so populous . . ."[12] Despite her efforts to rid the country, badly afflicted by hunger and poverty, of 'those kinde of people', by 1601 the problem was still felt to be so severe that the ageing Queen issued a Royal Proclamation ordering all 'blacka-moores' out of the kingdom.[13]

By the end of the sixteenth century London's black minority had become sufficiently large to cause the government concern. Yet it was Elizabeth's encouragement of the trade with Africa, from which she stood to gain financially, that brought about black immigration. Black servants were in the employ of royal favourites at Court and of others less well-placed.[14] Not all Africans were enslaved domestics. Some had gained their freedom and actively participated in their local churches.[15] Some were sufficiently independent to pay their own taxes[16] while a small minority even possessed property.[17] Within twenty years of Elizabeth's attempt to purge the country of its Africans, the black minority had firmly integrated itself into socially acceptable positions. Employment of Negroes as servants in early Stuart England—and once again after the Restoration in 1660—reinstated the Africans in the ranks from which Elizabeth had tried to dislodge them.[18] As trade with Africa grew, more and more Africans found employment on board British ships and this became more pronounced in the eighteenth century.[19]

However, it was events in the New World in the seventeenth century, namely the British settlement of the future sugar islands, which were responsible for the large-scale black immigration into Britain. As the human flotsam and jetsam of British Caribbean expansion Africans arrived in Britain, notably in London and Bristol, some in the home-coming ships, some brought as objects of curiosity, like other exotic African commodities or as profitable bounty for returning sailors; others as servants to the ships' captains and even as free, independent sailors.

Resurrecting lost people always presents technical problems for the historian. In the case of England's black minority, for instance, there is no accurate information which enables us to sketch in the dimensions of immigration and settlement. Because the black minority was largely enslaved and because it was consigned to the status of sub-human property, its members left behind few historical traces of their own creation. Names and dates scratched on decaying headstones, crude statistics in crumbling parish registers, cryptic advertisements in the small print of brown, flaking newspapers; these are some of the clues about England's black minority.

Newspaper advertisements, above all, give an insight into and the flavour of the pathetic world of the English slave. Year after year, newspapers across the country offered slaves for sale as they did any other commodity. Such advertisements, reflecting the inhumanity of the white host society, give a rare glimpse of the human characteristics of the slave. The shape, size, age, colour, dress and even peculiarities of the slaves are often only detectable through the medium of the advertisements which sought to sell them and we are able briefly to gaze at an individual face in the historical crowd.

Early in the eighteenth century it became apparent to contemporaries that the number of ex-slaves in Britain was growing, a fact which was taken to indicate a black threat to white employment. Of even greater concern was the ease with which incoming slaves left their masters and swelled the ranks of London's free, but poor, black community. In the West Indies there had been a close correlation between the colour of a man's skin and his occupational role in society. Immigrant slaves found this to be true no longer. For the first time they undertook similar work side by side with white servants. They were quick to realise that menial work was not the natural preserve of the Negro. They saw that white menials enjoyed certain conditions of labour denied to the Negro. This inequality of treatment produced dissatisfaction and a powerful desire among slaves to be free.[20] Many headed for the untouchable warrens and alleyways of poor London where a black community existed, on the riverside in Wapping and among the "blackbirds of St. Giles".

Among the free blacks in London there were strong, unmistakable signs of community and cohesive social behaviour. Isolated in pockets in an alien white city,[21] the slaves, from a multitude of tribal backgrounds, found a unity and collective self-help in the one factor which distinguished them above all from society at large: their colour. Even when they involved themselves in the institutions of the white man they tended to adapt it to their own needs and traditions. Thus a Negro baptism, itself popularly but mistakenly believed to confer automatic freedom on any slave, became a social occasion. Celebrations and festivities were often exclusively black, affording an opportunity in the security of a tavern for the Negroes to seal themselves off from society outside and to fall back on patterns of behaviour and expression which few Englishmen would have understood or appreciated. In general black community life tended to be beyond the sight and hearing of curious white society.[22]

For the free Negro in London the prime problems were physical survival and the dangers of recapture and repatriation to the slave colonies. Whatever the state of English law in relation to slavery only the luckiest and best-placed could hope to seek redress for his recapture on the streets of London. Once kidnapped and imprisoned on board a ship at anchor in the Thames it was only a matter of time before the unfortunate Negro would be sold on the quayside of a West Indian port.[23] There is no way of assessing the numbers forced back into slavery in this way but it is unlikely that they in any way made up for the large number of slaves who escaped.[24] All the evidence points to a rapid growth in the free black population in England. Immersed in a society where freedom, as opposed to slavery, was the norm, and aware of the existence of a free black community, whose members urged them to flee, newly arrived slaves experienced the exhilaration of sudden personal and collective awareness.

By 1772 contemporaries reckoned that some 15,000 Negroes lived in London.[25] Of greatest concern to the host society in general and to the absentee planters in particular, who constantly lost their black property on the streets of London, was the sheer size of the black population and the threat it was thought to pose to the social order. They were disturbed by the thought of miscegenation, a prospect both real and immediate since an estimated two-thirds of the Negroes were young males. It was impossible for all of them to form monogamous relations with women of African descent and inevitable that many would settle with English women of their own social level. Ironically, the most bitter comments came from absentee planters, who in the West Indies bore responsibility for the growth of a brown mulatto class. Closely tied to the fear of miscegenation was an implicit fear of black sexuality, a fear which, in its turn, was related to long-standing rumours about the size of the African male's sex organs. The anxiety, apparent earlier in the eighteenth century, that free blacks posed a threat to the Englishman's job opportunities, grew in proportion to the expansion of the black population.

The free black community in London was severely circumscribed in its freedom. Those slaves who fled their masters' control found their only refuge in that nether world of poverty which characterised pre-industrial London, a freedom to be survived rather than enjoyed. Certain former slaves did succeed, by dint of effort and fortuitous contacts, to rise from the general level in which freed slaves found themselves. Three men in particular, from different African and slave backgrounds, were adopted by white society as representatives of their community. Cugoano, Ignatius Sancho and Equiano came to speak for that mass of Negroes, in London and in the West Indies, who were muted by their circumstances.[26] These men were lionised by polite society to whom they represented a certain ideal type of African: the kind of successful, religious and slightly precious social aspirant who could adorn the salons of London with his unusual colour. In an age when the African was overwhelmingly regarded as sub-human the presence of free, literate Negroes who spoke up for their community offered a rallying point and a reference for those, both black and white, who sought to reinstate the African. Even where they merely repeated the words of white humanitarians, their impact was greater because theirs was the voice of personal experience. Furthermore, in their own achievements they offered a living contradiction to the widely held belief that the African was incapable of 'improvement'.

Ignatius Sancho, perhaps the best known of the prominent free Africans, was born on board a slaver in mid-Atlantic and brought to England at the age of two. A friend of Garrick and Sterne, he moved on the fringes of Johnsonian London. His letters, published in 1780 after his death, pressed on his friends the situation of his black brethren. The impact of these letters is indicated by the extent of their sales. The subscription list for the first edition was said to have been longer than any other since the launching of the *Spectator* fifty years before.[27]

More impressive intellectually than Sancho, Ottobah Cugoano, a Fante by birth, published his *Thoughts and Sentiments* in 1787.[28] His book was impressive for the illuminating comparison he drew between British and African society. Much of the British 'anthropological' view of West Africa was a strange assortment of facts wrapped in rumour and myth. Cugoano's achievement lay in giving the reading public an African insight into African society.

Sancho, Cugoano and Equiano all relied heavily upon Biblical inspiration and terminology for their writing, a fact which gave their writings credibility. The degree of religious zeal in these men, all members of the established church, is an indication of the black community's commitment to the white man's religion; but a distinction must be drawn between the impact of *theology* upon the slaves and the impact of the framework of church organisation. The non-conformist churches in particular offered a medium and a structure through which the slaves could organise themselves.[29] Certain church organisations were feared as giving the slaves a means of collective organisation and action. Such fears turned out to be justified because these factors helped to cause serious slave unrest in the West Indies in the early nineteenth century. However, London's black community in the eighteenth century showed no signs of growing radical awareness through the medium of church organisation. Indeed, those elements of Christianity absorbed by London's black community acted rather as a brake on black unrest. Far from reaching for those Christian tenets which asserted the rights and equality of all men, the free black community and their spokesmen clung to the distant hope of future salvation. Religion may have introduced a ray of hope into their wretched world but at the same time it had a socially pacifying effect.

On the conclusion of the American War of Independence in

1783 ex-slaves who had fought on the losing British side in return for offers of freedom were transported to Britain where they joined the lines of black beggars in the streets of London. The social conditions of these unfortunates produced disquiet, and charitable humanitarians were unable to cope with the excessive demands upon their limited resources. Inspired largely by Granville Sharp, a scheme emerged to recruit London's poor Negroes and to ship them 'home', with Government help, to Sierra Leone where they would settle as an agricultural community. The indigenous poor had long been one of the commonest sights in the capital. But, in this instance, society moved to deal with the contemporary black problem and not with the question of poverty. Elizabeth had ordered the Negroes to be expatriated. This solution was suggested again in 1787 and put forward moreover this time by the friends of the black community. But, however good the design or intention of the scheme, it failed utterly to succeed. The prospect of life in Sierra Leone attracted no more than a few hundred, a number scarcely likely to diminish the 'problem'. The transportation and equipping of the expedition gave scope for further exploitation of hapless, innocent people. When they arrived the settlers found the land inhospitable and their freedom at risk from slave traders. Those lucky enough to survive the ravages of the first year were abandoned by their white leaders. News of the appalling experiences of the settlers soon reached the black community in London—indeed their sufferings actually began on board ship in the Thames.[30] Cugoano complained bitterly about their treatment and noted that news of the undertaking was unlikely to encourage further emigration from London.

Organisers of the Sierra Leone settlement had employed Equiano as a respectable link-man with the black community but his battle against the corruptions of the undertaking swiftly led to his dismissal. Equiano was insistent and made representations at the highest level of government. Selection of Equiano in the first instance is an indication of his prominence in London in the mid-1780s; he was respected, vocal and well-placed.[31] His autobiography, published in 1789, went through

eight editions in five years and reached an even wider readership than Sancho's letters. In it he argued strongly that African
society ought not to be dismissed or scorned because it failed to
comply with European norms but that it should be studied,
understood and appreciated on its own terms. Equiano, relying
on memories of his African childhood, gave the reader a wealth
of hard, anthropological detail about West Africa. This was
important, for few Englishmen could understand Africans in
terms of their own culture and environment. The Africans
whom Englishmen were accustomed to deal with, in the West
Indies and in Britain, were those brutalised by the experiences
of the middle passage and plantation life. These experiences,
such as the break-up of family and tribal structures, the denial
of religion, and the general cultural deprivation were designed
deliberately, with some success, to rob the African of initiative
and talent superfluous to the life of a slave. Moreover, much of
the information about the Negro was propagated by the
venomous hacks employed by the slave lobby. Equiano's
greatest contribution lay in restoring, if only impressionistically,
some of the human dimensions of the African.

There existed, however, very distinct if far from accurate
concepts about Africa in the English mind even before the
harsh facts and realities of that continent forced themselves
into the English awareness. The scriptures contained a multitude of references to the existence and condition of black
humanity. In an age when information derived from the
scriptures possessed a widespread social importance, Biblical
explanation offered a reference against which the observable
facts of life were measured.[32] Whole sections of the population
acquired what little education they possessed through the
medium of scriptural writings. Even the educated and literate
minority were instructed to a large degree from Biblical or
classical sources.

In the fifteenth and sixteenth centuries a second source of
information emerged. Published narratives of adventurous
voyages became hugely successful. Mandeville's *Travels*,[33] for

example, widely read in manuscript form from the 1360s, drew together in a convincing web of fabrication most of the truths, Biblical snippets and classical references which had been common currency for centuries. The credibility of these accounts lay in the author's claims of personal experience. "Trow all this for sickerly I saw it with mine eyes and mickle more than I have told you." Mandeville regaled his reader with amazing tales of Asia, India, Amazonia and Ethiopia. Perhaps the first great romantic travel story, it told of the Kingdom of Prester John, somewhere in the interior of Africa, where the land flowed with milk and honey and the rivers with precious jewels. It was in fact both fictional and allegorical but by the sixteenth century Mandeville's story had become convincing reality in the minds of the readership. In the fifteenth and sixteenth centuries there developed between writers of travel accounts a process of literary cannibalism and Mandeville suffered the fate he had subjected others to: his work was seized upon by later writers for the 'facts' it contained.

From the mid-sixteenth century, however, as Africans were brought to London and as English trading contacts with Africa increased and prospered, more evidence about Africa was available. Yet, far from challenging the legacy of mythology about that continent, it was to a large extent incorporated into that mythology. Elizabethan sailors and traders, when confronted with intriguing aspects of African life which they were unable to explain, fell back on the mythology which had already so conditioned their image of the African. British writers, stimulated by the growth in knowledge about Africa sought to explain the African's colour, origins and social life. It was the blackness of Africa which intrigued and challenged English writers more than any social characteristic, and black Africans were gathering in London at a time when contemporary social values found expression in concepts of whiteness and purity. The Queen's "pale beauty" and virginity were qualities fostered by the Monarch herself.

A direct line can be drawn in the English interpretation of the Negro from Mandeville's *Travels* to Thomas Carlyle's violently negrophobic *Discourse on the Nigger Question*, published in 1849. He said nothing new, unusual or unique; his interpretation, given a new twist by the collapse of the sugar colonies, contained many of the ingredients of mythology and caricature of the previous three centuries. From the mid-eighteenth century however, this tradition of caricaturing the Negro for the English reading public was given a new urgency by the need of the slave-owners to resist what they saw as an encroaching, corrosive tide of philanthropy.

Propaganda in favour of the English involvement in slavery had emerged naturally with the growth in the economic importance of the slave trade. But it intensified as opposition to the institution of slavery developed. From the 1760s a paper war broke out between the slave lobby and the philanthropists in which the enslaved African was presented in such a caricatured form—sometimes even by his friends—as to become almost unrecognisable to those who knew him. To the supporters of slavery the Negro remained an inferior species whose manifest inequality could be proved simply by reference to any of the well-known and widely accepted 'facts' of African life. To many of the philanthropists the African was an innocent child of nature, a noble savage, corrupted and debased by the European. The friends of the Negro often tended to put forward a stereotype whose characteristics and features owed more to the romantic vision of the beholder than to African reality.

Of the two views, that purveyed by the slave lobby was, until the later eighteenth century, much the more influential. This plantocratic case frequently received help from unexpected quarters. The views of David Hume, for example, achieved wide publicity and added strength to the planters' argument. "I am apt to suspect the Negroes . . . to be naturally inferior to the Whites. There never was a civilised nation of any other complexion than white, or even any individual eminent either in action or speculation. No ingenious manufacturer among them, no arts, no sciences. There are Negro slaves dispersed all over Europe, of which none ever discovered any symptom of ingenuity."[34] That Hume, an educated, sophisticated man should choose to ignore the evidence contradicting this view and instead contribute to the perpetuation of mythology indicates that the prejudices often stemmed not from the ignorant but from the informed and enlightened.

Planters and their propagandists searched for evidence which both justified their involvement with slavery and placed the African beyond the pale of English comprehension. The writings of Edward Long and Bryan Edwards exemplified this kind of literature. Both men were quite exceptional and their books, which are in themselves classics of colonial history, are of a much superior quality to the cheap pamphlets which flooded the reading public in the eighteenth century. Their writings were imbued with the plantocratic philosophy. The major themes, occurring time and again in their caricatures of the Negro were the African's blackness and 'animal' features, his alleged indolence and untrustworthiness and his unusual sexual powers. Long, for instance, referred to the features of the Negro to prove the African's relationship to the orang-outan. This tactic had long been effective in reducing the African to an absurd level and in the hands of Edward Long the device became more successful because of the author's fame and influence.

Long was most deeply concerned by what he took to be black indolence. Remove the constraints of slavery, he alleged, and the black would revert to type, picking fruit from the trees while happily watching the collapse of the plantations. This theme occurs again in the works of Carlyle and Trollope. The collapse of the sugar colonies in the 1840s, when thousands of former slaves left the plantations for the marginal existence of squatters and small producers, gave an added dimension to the old myths about the Negro. For Carlyle and Trollope, emancipation was seen to prove the planters' assertions of black indolence, unreliability and anti-social behaviour. Bryan Edwards, too, was deeply disturbed about the fate of the plantations and while his vision of the Negro was similar, it lacked the asperity and hate so obvious in Long. However, both men described with great emphasis the lust and brutality which, they claimed, marked black slave sexuality. This emphasis can of course be traced back to the early narratives. To the evidence of African familial and tribal relations, however, the planters added evidence of the patterns of sexual behaviour of slaves in the New World. From this they alleged that the Negro had an appetite for unnatural and excessive sexual experiences and that he had no capacity for the refined and tender feelings of the white man. "If by love is meant that tender attachment to one individual object, which in civilised life is desire heightened by sentiment, and refined by delicacy, I doubt if it ever found a place in the African bosom."[35]

Despite emancipation, this caricature of the Negro became accepted truth by the mid-nineteenth century and was to facilitate the development of racial prejudice during the course of the British imperial expansion of the late nineteenth century.

Slavery and the slave trade, as economic and commercial institutions, had the backing of the force of law. In the colonies of the Caribbean and mainland America new laws were born of the planters' need to give legal sanction to the slave society they had created. For most of the eighteenth century they controlled the local assemblies, dictating the nature of legislation. They also acted as law enforcement officers.[36] The British Parliament, by comparison, introduced no special legislation for the regulation of slavery in England. This was due primarily to the relative unimportance of slavery in England, although in the last quarter of the eighteenth century, with the growth of a free black community, powerful voices called for special legislation to defend the slave-owners' interests. Despite the absence of such legislation the institution of slavery flourished in England. Somehow or other, therefore, a legal framework had to be created to deal with slavery. While it is true that a form of slavery had existed in England in the early Middle Ages, it had left no trace in English law save an occasional reference to 'freemen' and 'villeins'.

Analysis of the relationship between English law and slavery reveals an ambivalence between the need to defend vested economic interests while simultaneously underwriting certain human rights. Slavery in this sense was an institution which pulled in opposite directions. On the one hand it was a powerful economic system upon which depended much of the nation's wealth; on the other it entailed a crude loss of liberty, the likes of which had not been seen in England for centuries. Whenever faced with problems of slavery in England, the courts swung violently in their interpretations, depending on which of these two elements in slavery they sought to uphold. They were not rescued from this embarrassment until the total emancipation of 1834.

At the time when slaves were arriving in England in ever increasing numbers, when slaves could be bought and sold openly through the medium of newspapers, William Blackstone, the foremost commentator on English law in the eighteenth century, pronounced that ". . . the spirit of Liberty is so deeply implanted in our constitution, and rooted even in our very soil, that a slave or a negro, the moment he lands in England, falls under the protection of the laws, and so far becomes a freeman; though the master's rights to his services may possibly still continue."[37] Soon after he first published this opinion, Blackstone received representations from the court of King's Bench pointing out that this opinion had no basis in law.[38]

Blackstone was not alone in his view; there was widespread support for the notion that slavery could not legally exist in England. A famous Evangelist, writing in 1768, noted that "the British laws disown perpetual servitude. . . . The right of the planter to his Negro is only founded on the acts of his provincial assembly."[39] The welter of English legislation which lay like a cocoon around the institution of slavery was not designed to foster and encourage slavery in England; it provided for the English slaving presence in West Africa, on the high seas and in the plantation colonies. While the brutalities of colonial slave codes threw the moderation of domestic English slavery into sharp relief, it ought not to be thought that English law never made provision for slavery. The legality of domestic slavery rested not on statutory law, that is, specific legislation, but on case law (precedents of decided cases), legal opinions, and confusing references to earlier types of English villeinage.

In 1569 an English court held that since slavery could not exist in England, compensation could not be recovered for the loss of the person of a slave.[40] A century later a contrary view was expressed: ". . . Negroes being usually bought and sold among Merchants, so Merchandise, and also being Infidels, there might be Property in them . . ."[41] There was not, however, a clear-cut victory for the slave lobby. Throughout the eighteenth century English courts contradicted and overruled earlier verdicts in a display of unhappy indecision, as they wrestled with the changing contours of domestic slavery. At one point a legal decision seemed to hold out freedom to the black community, only for freedom to be snatched away as another court reached an opposite conclusion. Baptism, for example, was widely believed to confer freedom on a slave until an English court pronounced that: "If baptism should be accounted a manumission, it would very much endanger the trade of the plantations, which cannot be carried on without the help and labour of these slaves."[42]

Pressure from slaveowners for watertight legal approval of English slavery led to the famous opinion of 1729 which effectively crushed black hopes of freedom until the euphoria of 1772. The Attorney and Solicitor Generals, Philip Yorke and Charles Talbot, when asked for an opinion on the legality of slavery in England, firmly denied the ". . . vulgar error, that slaves become free by their being in England or Ireland, or from being baptised."[43] The opinion was simple and clear-cut. In it, to use the words of Lord Mansfield in 1772, both men "pledged themselves to the British planters for all the legal consequences of slaves coming over to this kingdom or being baptised."[44] In the 43 years after 1729 further decisions added more confusion to the situation. In 1749 Lord Hardwicke, the former Philip Yorke, confirmed his opinion of 1729,[45] but in 1762 Lord Chancellor Henley noted: "As soon as a man sets foot on English ground he is free."[46]

It was the famous Mansfield judgement of June 22 1772 which signalled, for contemporaries and historians alike, the final freeing of England's slaves. Mansfield held that no master could forcibly take a slave back to the colonies against the slave's wishes. The circumstances of the case were simple. In 1769 a certain Mr Stewart sailed from Virginia to England with his slave Somerset. On arrival, Somerset ran away. Recaptured, he was consigned to a ship sailing for Jamaica where his master intended to sell him. Somerset's friends and Granville Sharp, the English philanthropist, challenged Stewart and the ship's captain on a writ of Habeas Corpus.[47] Already Sharp had freed half a dozen slaves by this technique but in this instance he was seeking, not merely Somerset's freedom, but a firm judgement which would establish the general freedom of all slaves in England, something he had tried, but failed, to achieve in the Strong case of 1767.[48]

Mansfield, in the court of King's Bench, delayed judgement for five months, during which time an enormous groundswell of popular interest built up in the 'Negro case'. In the course of comment in the press and pamphlet literature the narrow legal issue in the case was interpreted on all sides to be the larger question of the freedom of England's black community. Mansfield resisted the drift of events and tried to persuade both sides to settle the case out of court, so removing from his shoulders the burden of deciding on an issue fraught with difficult social repercussions. Failing to do this, Mansfield made it clear in court and, thirteen years later in another case, that his task was more restricted than most people thought; namely, whether or not to sustain the writ or to allow the forcible extradition of a slave by his master.[49]

The final hearing lived up to expectation. It became a battle between the concepts of freedom and slavery. Somerset's case, presented by five counsel led by Francis Hargrave, was—and remains—a classic analysis of the legal principles and precedents involved in the question of English slavery. Weighing on the minds of all participants was the prospect of a wider freedom for the whole black community. "The setting 14,000 or 15,000 men at once loose by a solemn opinion, is very disagreeable in the effects it threatens." Mansfield attempted to dodge these effects by confining the issue to a narrow point of law. "The only question before us is, whether the cause on the return is sufficient? If it is not he must be discharged."[50] The decision was seized upon as establishing total freedom for the black community, but in 1785 Mansfield commented that ". . . the public were generally mistaken in the determination of the court of King's Bench, in the case of Somerset the negro, which had often been quoted, for nothing more was then determined, than that there was no right in the master forcibly to take the slave and carry him abroad."[51] The only contemporary law report to deal with the case was drawn up in 1776, four years after the hearing, by the well-known radical Capel Lofft. Time clearly distorted his memory for his version of Mansfield's summing-up contained those wider implications of the case which had in fact been presented not by Mansfield, but by Hargrave. This transposition and the general interpretation of the case assumed the authority of accepted truth in a variety of slave cases, particularly in America.[52]

Nonetheless the decision, for all its limitations, narrowed down the legal options of the slave-owners.[53] But, whatever the legal consequences, the fact remains that long after 1772 slaves continued to be bought and sold and re-exported to the colonies from England.[54] The planters dealt with the new situation by requiring slaves accompanying them from the colonies to sign an indenture. Thus, on arrival in England the slave was converted, for the duration of the visit, into an indentured servant who was compelled by the terms of the indenture to return with his master to the colonies where he would revert to his former status as a slave.[55] New black arrivals after 1772 were, in strict legal terms, therefore, more tightly shackled to their masters than they had been previously.

Gradually, however, from the 1780s, the status of the Negro in England improved, not so much because of stronger legal safeguards but because of changing social patterns and an improvement in popular attitudes towards the black community. With the growth of humanitarian sympathy at many social levels it became easier for Negroes to seize and to defend their freedom. Abolition of the slave trade in 1807 made slaves too scarce and expensive in the West Indies for planters to

B

import them into England as retainers, particularly when it was apparent that runaway slaves received more public sympathy and help than the aggrieved planters. Foreigners in the early nineteenth century commented on the benign nature of English racial attitudes[56] but freedom for the Negro in England could only be qualified as long as slavery remained lawful in the Empire.

A series of economic changes, which pushed the plantation economies into the second rank of economic importance for Britain, paralleled and reinforced a highly effective campaign waged by two generations of philanthropists and led to the abolition of the slave trade in 1807 and full emancipation in 1834.[57] In the 1760s all the evidence suggests that the humanitarian impulse was felt by only a minority; by the 1790s when the first wave of popular English radicalism shook the foundations of stable government, emancipation and international brotherhood had entered into the daily political currency of artisans and ordinary working men right across the nation. In a movement rooted in the Rights of Man, the rights of all men, black and white, were not forgotten and even when the battle for domestic reform was at its height in the middle of the decade the English Jacobins never ignored the even greater injustices perpetrated against the Negro. In the last forty years of the eighteenth century philanthropy permeated English sensibilities and opened the way to abolition and emancipation.[58]

No single person was responsible for the success of the abolitionists but one man was pre-eminent. From the 1760s Granville Sharp harnessed his impressive funds of scholarship and influence to the daunting task of restoring to the black community its lost freedom and humanity. He cared for and sustained large numbers of London's poor and desperate Negroes; he wrote scholarly and popular tracts in their interests; and he challenged the slave owners, privately in face to face confrontations and publicly before the courts. Sharp drew together powerful friends and contacts to form an influential pressure group. In those early, frustrating years of the campaign, Sharp's work on behalf of the black community was monumental. Despite setbacks his constancy and determination sustained the cause of abolition at a time when slavery seemed to be sinking its roots deeper and deeper into English soil.

Granville Sharp belonged to that class of Englishmen whose wealth and influence rarely blinded them to the difficulties of maintaining the rights and liberties of other less fortunate men, be they American colonists, English artisans or black slaves. In the 1760s it was the appalling condition of Negroes in London which affected him so forcibly. He embarked on an educational campaign to eradicate slavery. His tracts and pamphlets taught the English the truth about slavery. It was, he claimed, a contagious virus which had travelled from the West Indies and America to England, inimical to the best traditions and even the economic interests of the English, without any foundation in scripture, law or custom.

As the century advanced more and more influential figures joined the abolitionist campaign. A corrective was needed to the planter's virtual monopoly in the dissemination of information about slavery and the Negro. The philanthropists were able to corrode this monopoly with the help of influential men who could command the hearing and respect of whole areas of the population. John Wesley, one such man, brought home the immorality and unchristian nature of slavery by portraying in vivid terms the subjugation of the African. "Notwithstanding ten thousand laws, right is right and wrong is wrong still." Coming from a man whose audience was unsurpassed late in the century, Wesley's pleas gave a shattering blow to the case for slavery. Wesley went behind the stereotyped image of the Negro, relating it to the slave experience. "Are not stubbornness, cunning, pilfering, and divers other vices the natural necessary fruits of slavery? . . . You kept them stupid and wicked, by cutting them off from all opportunities of improving, either in knowledge or virtue. And now you assign their want of wisdom and goodness as the reason for using them worse than brutes."[59]

In the last twenty years of the century the attack on slavery by churchmen became a notable feature of the abolitionist campaign. The scriptures had previously been used to sanction the existence of slavery. As philanthropy gained support the tables were turned. The slave lobby had to contend with scriptural arguments from scholars without equal among their own supporters. The Reverend James Ramsay, for example, found support for racial equality in the nature of the soul which was, he claimed, "a simple substance, not to be distinguished by squat or tall, black, brown or fair." Ramsay also pointed to Negroes who, when given the opportunity, had revealed talents which could never have emerged under slavery. Thomas Clarkson, a contemporary of his and one of the most active abolitionists, wrote a major tract, *An Essay on the Slavery and Commerce of the Human Species*, in which he isolated and demolished the arguments of the slave lobby. Whatever characteristics the Negro revealed, Clarkson wrote, they were a result of the warping effect of slavery. In Africa the talents and qualities exhibited by the inhabitants were those best suited to that society. Given the chance, as a free man, to develop those talents the English would recognise—in mechanics, commerce or the liberal arts—the Negro would be the equal of the European. Clarkson restored to the image of the African those personal and social attributes which long years of slavery and misrepresentation had destroyed.[60]

In 1823 William Wilberforce, the man who came to epitomise the humanitarian impulse from the 1790s until his death, still felt the need to comment ". . . that though the old prejudice, that the Negroes are creatures of inferior nature, is no longer maintained in terms, there is yet too much reason to fear that a latent impression arising from it still continues practically to operate in the colonies." Like his precursors Wilberforce seized on empirical evidence which tended to prove the equality and ultimate social 'perfectability' of the Negro. Freed from the shackles of slavery the Negroes in Sierra Leone, Trinidad and Haiti had more than justified the expectations of their white friends in England. This sort of evidence offered an alternative vision of the Negro. While the old caricature continued to haunt English literature—and Carlyle and Trollope should remind us of the strength of this tradition—it did so in severe competition with a school of thought whose central purpose was to demolish the stereotype for what it was: the crumbling prop of an immoral system.

From the 1840s the West Indies lost their economic utility to Britain and became instead a financial and administrative burden. The symptoms of decline were evident long before emancipation. The end of slavery merely accelerated a process long in train, of the replacement of the West Indies inside the British imperial economy by other areas of the world and other sources of materials and wealth. Having filled the islands with Africans and having drained the islands of the resulting wealth the British generated enough capital to stimulate self-sustaining growth at home and to diversify their economy. Investment normally funnelled into West Africa and the West Indies was diverted into new, more lucrative fields. The former slave colonies were left to drift into economic insignificance, until they became a wasteland. As the African in the West Indies became less important economically he became less an issue of social and political debate in England.[61] Until the fresh assaults on Africa late in the nineteenth century the English paid less heed to the economic and philosophical problems posed by black humanity, problems which, after three centuries, had died with the old slave empire.[62]

CHAPTER 1

The Impact of the African on English Thought

Long before the European encroachment on West Africa the blackness of the African occupied a special place in European curiosity about the continent. Before the fifteenth century, scriptural descriptions of the Negro's blackness, such as in the Song of Solomon and the book of Jeremiah, and classical references in Hippocrates, Pliny and Ptolemy, had been given widespread prominence. Even after, when men wished to offer new explanations for human blackness, the centuries of traditional explanation hung like a dead weight on their shoulders.

In England the debate about the cause of blackness raged well into the nineteenth century. Whereas in the course of the eighteenth century it soured and became stultified as it passed through the hands of the Grub Street hacks who were paid to write for both the philanthropist and slave lobbies, in the sixteenth and seventeenth centuries the same issue had much more freshness and immediacy. There was a distinctly exciting element in the intellectual debate about black Africans and the two selections presented here, parts of George Best's *Discourse* of 1578[1] and Sir Thomas Browne's *Enquiries into Vulgar and Common Errors* of 1646[2] give some indication of this.

Returning from his third voyage with Frobisher in 1578, George Best published his *Discourse* partly to prove that all regions of the world were habitable. Inevitably he was drawn

32

into a discussion about the problems of living in hot climates, which led to an analysis of the relationship between heat and human blackness. He said little about this question that had not been said before. Instead, he concentrated on disproving, to his own satisfaction, those theories which he found untenable and giving a brief exposition of the prevailing views as to the cause of the African's blackness. He thus presents us with a valuable synopsis of popular ideas on the subject. His book was immediately popular and was translated into Latin, French and Italian before being incorporated into the third edition of Hakluyt's travel commentaries in 1600.

Sir Thomas Browne (1605–1682) was a doctor of medicine, with degrees from Leyden and Oxford, an intellectual of international stature who, for all his learning and a cold penetrating mind, was never able to free himself completely from the popular superstitutions of his day. In 1646 he produced his great work, *Pseudodoxia Epimedica, or Enquiries into very many received tenets and commonly presumed truths, which examined prove but Vulgar and Common Errors.* Browne's *Enquiries* was the fruit of years of research and yet in it can be seen many of the self-same 'Common Errors' which he was intending to purge. Added to his encyclopaedic knowledge were the influences of magic and alchemy. The book itself is a fund of information; a massive far-reaching discussion in which the author happily moves through any topic which catches his intellectual attention. In dealing with the question of blackness he shows an impressive grasp of both classical and scientific material. After publication of the work Browne was firmly established in the reading public's estimate. He survived the Civil War and emerged after the Restoration as one of the country's foremost authorities on a wide range of scientific and academic subjects.

In his *Enquiries* Browne dealt with the traditional legends about the African with a critical mind which rejected their explanations for the African's blackness. His conclusions were not accepted in his lifetime but they cut through the corpus of myth about human blackness and elevated the question to the level of scientific investigation.

As the writings reproduced here suggest, when Englishmen tried to answer questions about the African they also touched upon issues which were profoundly political and religious. In the light of human evidence from Africa,[3] traditional explanations of the origins of mankind were open increasingly to the scrutiny of enquiring minds. It took no great leap of the imagination for the writer to stray from critical discussion about the African to critical discussion about the English. In talking about the Negro, the English began to look a little more critically at themselves and their values.

George Best, Discourse, 1578

Others againe imagine the middle Zone to be extreme hot, because the people of Africa, especially the Ethiopians, are so cole blacke, and their haire like wooll curled short, which blacknesse and curled haire they suppose to come onely by the parching heat of the Sunne, which how it should be possible I cannot see: for even under the Equinoctiall in America, and in the East Indies, and in the Ilands Moluccæ the people are not blacke, but tauney and white, with long haire uncurled as wee have, so that if the Ethiopians blacknesse came by the heat of the Sunne, why should not those Americans and Indians also be as blacke as they, seeing the Sunne is equally distant from them both, they abiding in one Parallel: for the concave and convexe Superficies of the Orbe of the Sunne is concentrike, and equidistant to the earth; except any man should imagine somewhat of Aux Solis, and Oppositum, which indifferently may be applied aswel to the one place as to the other. But the Sunne is thought to give no otherwise heat, but by way of Angle in reflection, and not by his neerenesse to the earth: for throughout all Africa, yea in the middest of the middle Zone, and in all other places upon the tops of mountaines there lyeth continuall snow, which is neerer to the Orbe of the Sunne, then the people are in the valley, by so much as the height of these mountaines amount unto, and yet the Sunne notwithstanding his neerenesse, can not melt the snow for want of convenient place of reflections. Also the middle region of the aire where all the haile, frost, and snow is engendred, is neerer unto the Sunne then the earth is, and yet there continueth perpetuall cold, because there is nothing that the Sunne beames may reflect against, whereby appeareth that the neerenesse of the body of the Sunne worketh nothing.

Therefore to returne againe to the blacke Moores. I my selfe have seene an Ethiopian as blacke as a cole brought into England, who taking a faire English woman to wife, begat a sonne in all respects as blacke as the father was, although England were his native countrey, and an English woman his mother: whereby it seemeth this blacknes proceedeth rather of some natural infection of that man, which was so strong, that neither the nature of the Clime, neither the good complexion of the mother concurring, coulde any thing alter, and therefore, wee cannot impute it to the nature of the Clime. And for a more fresh example, our people of Meta Incognita (of whom and for whom this discourse is taken in hande) that were brought this last yeere into England, were all generally of the same colour that many nations be, lying in the middest of the middle Zone. And this their colour was not onely in the face which was subject to Sunne and aire, but also in their bodies, which were stil covered with garments as ours are, yea the very sucking childe of twelve moneths age had his skinne of the very same colour that most have under the Equinoctiall, which thing cannot proceed by reason of the Clime, for that they are at least ten degrees more towardes the North then wee in England are, No, the Sunne never commeth neere their Zenith by fourtie degrees: for in effect, they are within three or foure degrees of that which they call the frosen Zone, and as I saide, fourtie degrees from the burning Zone, whereby it followeth, that there is some other cause then the Climate or the Sonnes perpendicular reflexion, that should cause the Ethiopians great blacknesse. And the most probable cause to my judgement is, that this blackenesse proceedeth of some naturall infection of the first inhabitants of that Countrey, and so all the whole progenie of them descended, are still polluted with the same blot of infection. Therefore it shall not bee farre from our purpose, to examine the first originall of these blacke men, and howe by a lineall discent they have hitherto continued thus blacke.

It manifestly and plainely appeareth by holy Scripture, that after the generall inundation and overflowing of the earth, there remained no moe men alive but Noe and his three sonnes, Sem, Cham, and Japhet, who onely were left to possesse and inhabite the whole face of the earth: therefore all the sundry discents that until this present day have inhabited the whole earth, must needes come of the off-spring either of Sem, Cham, or Japhet, as the onely sonnes of Noe, who all three being white, and their wives also, by course of nature should have begotten and brought foorth white children. But the envie of our great and continuall enemie the wicked Spirite is such, that as hee coulde not suffer our olde father Adam to live in the felicitie and Angelike state wherein hee was first created, but tempting him, sought and procured his ruine and fall: so againe, finding at this flood none but a father and three sonnes living, hee so caused one of them to transgresse and disobey his fathers commaundement, that after him all his posteritie shoulde bee accursed. The fact of disobedience was this: When Noe at the commandement of God had made the Arke and entred therein, and the floud-gates of heaven were opened, so that the whole face of the earth, every tree and mountaine was covered with abundance of water, hee straitely commaunded his sonnes and their wives, that they should with reverence and feare beholde the justice and mighty power of God, and that during the time of the floud while they remained in the Arke, they should use continencie, and abstaine from carnall copulation with their wives: and many other precepts hee gave unto them, and admonitions touching the justice of God, in revenging sinne, and his mercie in delivering them, who nothing deserved it. Which good instructions and exhortations notwithstanding his wicked sonne Cham disobeyed, and being perswaded that the first childe borne after the flood (by right and Lawe of nature) should inherite and possesse all the dominions of the earth, hee contrary to his fathers commandement while they were yet in the Arke, used company with his wife, and craftily went about thereby to dis-inherit the off-spring of his other two brethren: for the which wicked and detestable fact, as an example for contempt of Almightie God, and disobedience of parents, God would a sonne should bee borne whose name was Chus, who not onely it selfe, but all his posteritie after him should bee so blacke and lothsome, that it might remaine a spectacle of disobedience to all the worlde. And of this blacke and cursed Chus came all these blacke Moores which are in Africa, for after the water was vanished from off the face of the earth, and that the lande was dry, Sem chose that part of the land to inhabite in, which nowe is called Asia, and Japhet had that which now is called Europa, wherein wee dwell, and Africa remained for Cham and his blacke sonne Chus, and was called Chamesis after the fathers name, being perhaps a cursed, dry, sandy, and unfruitfull ground, fit for such a generation to inhabite in.

Thus you see, that the cause of the Ethiopians blacknesse is the curse and naturall infection of blood, and not the distemperature of the Climate; Which also may bee prooved by this example, that these blacke men are found in all parts of Africa, as well without the Tropickes, as within, even unto Capo de buona Speranza Southward, where, by reason of the Sphere, should be the same temperature that is in Sicilia, Morea and Candie, where al be of very good complexions. Wherefore I conclude, that the blacknesse proceedeth not of the hotenesse of the Clime, but as I saide, of the infection of blood, and therefore this their argument gathered of the Africans blacknesse is not able to destroy the temperature of the middle Zone.

Sir Thomas Browne, Enquiries into Vulgar and Common Errors, 1646

Of the Blackness of Negroes

It is evident not only in the general frame of Nature, that things most manifest unto sense, have proved obscure unto the understanding: But even in proper and appropriate Objects, wherein we affirm the sense cannot err, the faculties of reason most often fail us. Thus of colours in general, under whose gloss and vernish all things are seen, few or none have yet beheld the true nature; or positively set down their incontroulable causes.

... Why some men, yea and they a mighty and considerable part of mankind, should first acquire and still retain the gloss and tincture of blackness? Which whoever strictly enquires, shall find no less of darkness in the cause, than blackness in the effect it self; there arising unto examination no such satisfactory and unquarrelable reasons, as may confirm the causes generally received; which are but two in number: the heat and scorch of the Sun; or the curse of God on Cham and his Posterity.

The first was generally received by the Ancients, who in obscurities had no higher recourse than unto Nature, as may appear by a discourse concerning this point in Strabo. By Aristotle it seems to be implied in those Problems which enquire why the Sun makes men black, and not the fire? Why it whitens wax, yet blacks the skin? By the word *Æthiops* it self, applied to the memorablest Nations of Negroes, that is of a burnt and torrid countenance. The fancy of the Fable infers also the Antiquity of the opinions; which deriveth this complexion from the deviation of the Sun, and the conflagration of all things under Phaeton. But this opinion though generally embrased, was I perceive rejected by Aristobulus a very ancient Geographer; as is discovered by Strabo. It hath been doubted by several modern Writers, particularly by Ortelius; but amply and satisfactorily discussed as we know by no man. We shall therefore endeavour a full delivery hereof, declaring the grounds of doubt, and reasons of denial, which rightly understood, may, if not overthrow, yet shrewdly shake the security of this Assertion.

And first, Many which countenance the opinions in this reason, do tacitly and upon consequence overthrow it in another. For whilst they make the River Senage to divide and bound the Moors, so that on the South-side they are black, and on the other only tawny; they imply a secret causality herein from the air, place or river; and seem not to derive it from the Sun, the effects of whose activity are not precipitously abrupted, but gradually proceed to their cessations.

Secondly, If we affirm that this effect proceeded, or as we will not be backward to concede, it may be advanced and fomented from the fervour of the Sun; yet do we not hereby discover a principle sufficient to decide the question concerning other animals; nor doth he that affirmeth the heat makes man black, afford a reason why other animals in the same habitations maintain a constant and agreeable hue unto those in other parts, as Lions, Elephants, Camels, Swans, Tigers, Estriges, which though in Æthiopia, in the disadvantage of two Summers, and perpendicular Rayes of the Sun, do yet make good the complexion of their species, and hold a colourable correspondence unto those in milder regions. Now did this complexion proceed from heat in man, the same would be communicated unto other animals which equally participate the Influence of the common Agent.

Thirdly, If the fervour of the Sun, or intemperate heat of clime did solely occasion this complexion, surely a migration or change thereof might cause a sensible, if not a total mutation; which notwithstanding experience will not admit. For Negroes transplanted, although into cold and flegmatick habitations, continue their hue both in themselves, and also their generations; except they mix with different complexions; whereby notwithstanding there only succeeds a remission of their tinctures; there remaining unto many descents a strong shadow of their Originals; and if they preserve their copulations entire, they still maintain their complexions. As is very remarkable in the dominions of the Grand Signior, and most observable in the Moors in Brasilia, which transplanted about an hundred years past, continue the tinctures of their fathers unto this day. And so likewise fair or white people translated in hotter Countries receive not impressions amounting to this complexion, as hath been observed in many Europeans who have lived in the land of Negroes: and as Edvardus Lopes testifieth of the Spanish plantations, that they retained their native complexions unto his days.

Fourthly, If the fervour of the Sun were the sole cause hereof in Ethiopia or any land of Negroes; it were also reasonable that Inhabitants of the same latitude, subjected unto the same vicinity of the Sun, the same diurnal arch, and direction of its rayes, should also partake of the same hue and complexion, which notwithstanding they do not. For the Inhabitants of the same latitude in Asia are of a different complexion, as are the Inhabitants of Cambogia and Java, insomuch that some conceive the Negro is properly a native of Africa, and that those places in Asia inhabited now by Moors, are but the intrusions of Negroes arriving first from Africa, as we generally conceive of Madagascar, and the adjoyning Islands, who retain the same complexion unto this day. But this defect is more remarkable in America; which although subjected unto both the Tropicks, yet are not the Inhabitants black between, or near, or under either: neither to the South-ward in Brasilia, Chili, or Peru; nor yet to the North-ward in Hispaniola, Castilia del Oro, or Nicaragua. And although in many parts thereof there be at present swarms of Negroes serving under the Spaniard, yet were they all transported from Africa, since the discovery of Columbus; and are not indigenous or proper natives of America.

Fifthly, We cannot conclude this complexion in Nations from the vicinity or habitude they hold unto the Sun; for even in Africa they be Negroes under the Southern Tropick, but are not all of this hue either under or near the Northern. So the people of Gualata, Agades, Garamantes, and of Goaga, all within the Northern Tropicks, are not Negroes; but on the other side about Capo Negro, Cefala, and Madagascar, they are of a jetty black. . . .

Sixthly, And which is very considerable, there are Negroes in Africa beyond the Southern Tropick, and some so far removed from it, as Geographically the clime is not intemperate, that is, near the Cape of good Hope, in 36 of the Southern Latitude. Whereas in the same elevation Northward, the Inhabitants of America are fair; and they of Europe in Candy, Sicily, and some parts of Spain, deserve not properly so low a name as Tawny.

Lastly, Whereas the Africans are conceived to be more

peculiarly scorched and torrified from the Sun, by addition of driness from the soil, from want and defect of water; it will not excuse the doubt. For the parts which the Negroes possess, are not so void of Rivers and moisture, as is presumed; for on the other side the mountains of the Moon, in that great tract called Zanzibar, there are the mighty Rivers of Suama, and Spirito Santo; on this side, the great River Zaire, the mighty Nile and Niger; which do not only moisten and contemperate the air by their exhalations, but refresh and humectate the earth by their annual Inundations. . . .

Thus having evinced, at least made dubious, the Sun is not the Author of this Blackness, how, and when this tincture first began is yet a Riddle, and positively to determine, it sur-passeth my presumption. Seeing therefore we cannot discover what did effect it, it may afford some piece of satisfaction to know what might procure it. It may be therefore considered, whether the inward use of certain waters or fountains of peculiar operations, might not at first produce the effect in question.

Secondly, It may be perpended whether it might not fall out the same way that Jacob's cattle became speckled, spotted and ring-straked, that is, by the Power and Efficacy of Imagination; which produceth effects in the conception correspondent unto the phancy of the Agents in generation; and sometimes assimi-lates the Idea of the Generator into a reality in the thing in-gendred. For, hereof there pass for current many indisputed examples; so in Hippocrates we read of one, that from an intent view of a Picture conceived a Negro; And in the History of Heliodore of a Moorish Queen, who upon aspection of the Picture of Andromeda, conceived and brought forth a fair one. And thus perhaps might some say was the beginning of this complexion: induced first by Imagination, which having once impregnated the seed, found afterward concurrent co-opera-tions, which were continued by Climes, whose constitution advantaged the first impression. Thus Plotinus conceiveth white Peacocks first came in. Thus many opinion that from aspection of the Snow, which lieth long in Northern Regions, and high mountains, Hawks, Kites, Beares, and other creatures become white; and by this way Austin conceiveth the devil provided, they never wanted a white spotted Ox in Egypt; for such an one they worshipped, and called Apis.

Thirdly, It is not indisputable whether it might not proceed from such a cause and the like foundation of Tincture, as doth the black Jaundise, which meeting with congenerous causes might settle durable inquinations, and advance their generations unto that hue, which was naturally before but a degree or two below it. And this transmission we shall the easier admit in colour, if we remember the like hath been effected in organical parts and figures; the Symmetry whereof being casually or purposely perverted; their morbosities have vigorously descended to their posterities, and that in durable deformities. . . .

Lastly, If we still be urged to particularities, and such as declare how and when the seed of Adam did first receive this tincture; we may say that men became black in the same manner that some Foxes, Squirrels, Lions, first turned of this complexion, whereof there are a constant sort in divers Countries; that some Chaughs came to have red Legs and Bils, that Crows became pyed: All which mutations however they began, depend on durable foundations; and such as may continue for ever. And if as yet we must farther define the cause and manner of this mutation, we must confess, in matters of Antiquity, and such as are decided by History, if their Originals and first beginnings escape a due relation, they fall into great obscurities, and such as future Ages seldom reduce unto a resolution.

However therefore this complexion was first acquired, it is evidently maintained by generation, and by the tincture of the skin as a spermatical part traduced from father unto Son; so that they which are strangers contract it not, and the Natives which transmigrate, omit it not without commixture, and that after divers generations. And this affection (if the story were true) might wonderfully be confirmed, by what Maginus and others relate of the Emperour of Æthiopia, or Prester John, who, derived from Solomon, is not yet descended into the hue of his Country, but remains a Mulatto, that is, of a Mongril complexion unto this day. Now although we conceive this blackness to be seminal, yet are we not of Herodotus' conceit, that their seed is black. An opinion long ago rejected by Aristotle, and since by sense and enquiry. His assertion against the Historian was probable, that all seed was white; that is without great controversie in viviparous Animals, and such as have Testicles, or preparing vessels wherein it receives a manifest dealbation. And not only in them, but (for ought I know) in Fishes, not abating the seed of Plants; whereof at least in most though the skin and covering be black, yet is the seed and fructifying part not so: as may be observed in the seeds of Onyons, Pyonie and Basil. Most controvertible it seems in the spawn of Frogs, and Lobsters, whereof notwithstanding at the very first the spawn is white, contracting by degrees a blackness, answerable in the one unto the colour of the shell, in the other unto the Porwigle or Tadpole; that is, that Animall which first proceedeth from it. And thus may it also be in the generation and sperm of Negroes; that being first and in its naturals white, but upon separation of parts, accidents before invisible become apparent; there arising a shadow or dark efflorescence in the out-side; whereby not only their legitimate and timely births, but their abortions are also dusky, before they have felt the scorch and fervor of the Sun.

A second opinion there is, that this complexion was first a curse of God derived unto them from Cham, upon whom it was inflicted for discovering the nakedness of Noah. Which notwithstanding is sooner affirmed then proved, and carrieth with it sundry improbabilities. For first, if we derive the curse on Cham, or in general upon his posterity, we shall denigrate a greater part of the earth then was ever so conceived; and not only paint the Æthiopians and reputed sons of Cush, but the people also of Egypt, Arabia, Assyria and Chaldea; for by his race were these Countries also peopled. And if concordantly unto Berosus, the fragment of Cato *de Orignibus*, some things of Halicarnasseus, Macrobius, and out of them of Leandro and Annius, we shall conceive of the travels of Camese or Cham; we may introduce a generation of Negroes as high as Italy; which part was never culpable of deformity, but hath produced the magnified examples of beauty.

Secondly, The curse mentioned in Scripture was not denounced upon Cham, but Canaan his youngest son, and the reasons thereof are divers. The first, from the Jewish Tradition, whereby it is conceived, that Canaan made the discovery of the nakedness of Noah, and notified it unto Cham. Secondly, to have cursed Cham had been to curse all his posterity, whereof but one was guilty of the fact. And lastly, he spared Cham, because he had blessed him before. . . .

Thirdly, Although we should place the original of this curse upon one of the sons of Cham, yet were it not known from which of them to derive it. For the particularity of their descents is imperfectly set down by accountants, nor is it distinctly determinable from whom thereof the Æthiopians are proceeded. . . .

Fourthly, To take away all doubt or any probable divarication, the curse is plainly specified in the Text, nor need we dispute it, like the mark of Cain; *Servus servorum erit fratribus suis*, Cursed be Canaan, a servant of servants shall he be unto his brethren; which was after fulfilled in the conquest of Canaan, subdued by the Israelites, the posterity of Sem. . . .

Lastly, Whereas men affirm this colour was a Curse, I cannot make out the propriety of that name, it neither seeming so to them, nor reasonably unto us; for they take so much content therein, that they esteem deformity by other colours, describing the Devil, and terrible objects, white. And if we seriously consult the definitions of beauty, and exactly perpend what wise men determine thereof, we shall not apprehend a curse, or any deformity therein. For first, some place the essence thereof in the proportion of parts, conceiving it to consist in a comely commensurability of the whole unto the parts, and the parts between themselves: which is the determination of the best and learned Writers. Now hereby the Moors are not excluded from beauty: there being in this description no consideration of colours, but an apt connexion and frame of parts and the whole. Others there be, and those most in number, which place it not only in proportion of parts, but also in grace of colour. But to make Colour essential unto Beauty, there will arise no slender difficulty: For Aristotle in two definitions of pulchritude, and Galen in one, have made no mention of colour. Neither will it agree unto the Beauty of Animals: wherein notwithstanding there is an approved pulchritude. Thus horses are handsome under any colour, and the symmetry of parts obscures the consideration of complexions. Thus in concolour animals and such as are confined unto one colour, we measure not their Beauty thereby: for if a Crow or Black-bird grow white, we generally account it more pretty; And in almost a monstrosity descend not to opinion of deformity. By this way likewise the Moors escape the curse of deformity: there concurring no stationary colour, and sometimes not any unto Beauty.

The Platonick contemplators reject both these descriptions founded upon parts and colours, or either: as M. Leo the Jew hath excellently discoursed in his *Genealogy of Love*, defining beauty a formal grace, which delights and moves them to love which comprehend it. This grace say they, discoverable outwardly, is the resplendor and Ray of some interiour and invisible Beauty, and proceedeth from the forms of compositions amiable. Whose faculties if they can aptly contrive their matter, they beget in the subject an agreeable and pleasing beauty; if overruled thereby, they evidence not their perfections, but run into deformity. For seeing that out of the same materials, Thersites and Paris, Beauty and monstrosity may be contrived; the forms and operative faculties introduce and determine their perfections. Which in natural bodies receive exactness in every kind, according to the first Idea of the Creator, and in contrived bodies the phancy of the Artificer. And by this consideration of Beauty, the Moors also are not excluded, but hold a common share therein with all mankind.

Lastly, in whatsoever its Theory consisteth, or if in the general, we allow the common conceit of symmetry and of colour, yet to descend unto singularities, or determine in what symmetry or colour it consisted, were a slippery designation. For Beauty is determined by opinion, and seems to have no essence that holds one notion with all; that seeming beauteous unto one, which hath no favour with another; and that unto every one, according as custome hath made it natural, or sympathy and conformity of minds shall make it seem agreeable. Thus flat noses seem comely unto the Moor, an Aquiline or hawked one unto the Persian, a large and prominent nose unto the Romane; but none of all these are acceptable in our opinion. Thus some think it most ornamental to wear their Bracelets on their Wrests, others say it is better to have them about their Ancles; some think it most comely to wear their Rings and Jewels in the Ear, others will have them about their Privities; a third will not think they are compleat except they hang them in their lips, cheeks, or noses. Thus Homer to set off Minerva, calleth her gray or light-blew eyed: now this unto us seems far less amiable then the black. Thus we that are of contrary complexions accuse the blackness of the Moors as ugly: But the Spouse in the *Canticles* excuseth this conceit, in that description of hers, *I am black, but comely*. And howsoever Cerberus, and the furies of hell be described by the Poets under this complexion, yet in the beauty of our Saviour blackness is commended, when it is said, his locks are bushie and black as a Raven. So that to inferr this as a curse, or to reason it as a deformity, is no way reasonable; the two foundations of beauty, Symmetry and complexion receiving such various apprehensions; that no deviation will be expounded so high as a curse or undeniable deformity, without a manifest and confessed degree of monstrosity.

Lastly, It is a very injurious method unto Philosophy, and a perpetual promotion of ignorance, in points of obscurity; nor upon unto easie considerations, to fall upon a present refuge unto Miracles; or recurr unto immediate contrivance, from the insearchable hands of God. Thus in the conceit of the evil odor of the Jews, Christians without a farther research into the verity of the thing, or inquiry into the cause, draw up a judgement upon them from the passion of their Saviour. Thus in the wondrous effects of the clime of Ireland, and the freedom from all venemous creatures, the credulity of common conceit imputes this immunity until the benediction of S. Patrick, as Beda and Gyraldus have left recorded. Thus the Ass having a peculiar mark of a cross made by a black list down his back, and another athwart, or at right angles down his shoulders; common opinion ascribes this figure unto a peculiar signation; since that beast had the honour to bear our Saviour on his back. Certainly this is a course more desperate then Antipathies, Sympathies, or occult qualities; wherein by a final and satisfactive discernment of faith, we lay the last and particular effects upon the first and general cause of all things; whereas in the other, we do but palliate our determinations; untill our advanced endeavours do totally reject, or partially salve their evasions.

CHAPTER 2

The African Trade

"The West India and African trade are the most nationally beneficial of any we carry on," wrote one keen supporter of these trades in 1746. Linked together by the nature of European trade and colonial expansion from the sixteenth to the nineteenth centuries, West Africa and the New World yielded one indivisible trading nexus. By the early eighteenth century the term 'African trade' was synomous with 'slave trade' and its vital supporting services. In its origin, however, the European interest in West Africa was rooted not in the slaving potential but in the great variety of rare commodities the continent had to offer. With the expansion of the settlements on the far side of the Atlantic and the resultant demand for slave labour, it was the inhabitants themselves who became the most lucrative commodity in Africa.

The English were relatively late on the slaving scene, coming after the Portuguese and Spaniards. The making of inroads into the Iberian monopoly demanded personal daring and initiative allied to strong moral support from the home government. English traders had dabbled in slavery in a minor way before 1563,[1] but in that year the first organised English slave trading venture between West Africa and the West Indies was undertaken by John Hawkins (1532–1595), son of the famous William Hawkins.[2]

Steering a delicate course between legal and piratical ventures, Hawkins' first voyage was enormously successful.[3] It suggested to other traders and to the Elizabethan Court the enormous economic potential in slaving. It was to

48

be years before the English slave-trade ceased to be conducted in a haphazard and piratical fashion, partly because of the difficulties posed by the Iberian stranglehold on the Atlantic trades[4] and partly because the English lacked their own New World colonies until the seventeenth century. But Hawkins' first mission was of immediate and long term significance. It showed the potential, the method and the rewards of the African trade.

After the Restoration of Charles II the value of the African slave, both to the West Indian settlements and to Britain, was accepted generally. The Royal African Company was granted a monopoly for carrying on the slave trade in 1672.[5] With the rapid expansion of the plantation colonies however, and the consequent growth in demand for slave labour, the Company was unable to supply slaves in adequate numbers. It was deprived of its monopoly and continued trading only with difficulty. Postlewayt's tract,[6] reproduced below, was part of a campaign on behalf of the Company to recover its former monopoly position.[7] It emphasises the importance of the African trade to Britain as a whole, claiming that without the trade in Africans British industry would falter, the West Indian islands would not be able to survive and the fleet would be deprived of its training school.

With the emergence of the philanthropist lobby in the 1760s these claims came under fire increasingly. Partly as a response to the philanthropists, the slave lobby began, in the late eighteenth century, to produce literature such as the tract published by Richard Norris in 1789.[8] Extracts from this tract are reproduced below to illustrate the emphasis placed in this propaganda on the economic importance of the African slave. Abolish the slave trade, it was claimed, and the whole imperial economy would suffer.

The First Voyage of John Hawkins, 1562–1563

Master John Hawkins having made divers voyages to the Iles of the Canaries, and there by his good and upright dealing being growen in love and favour with the people, informed himselfe amongst them by diligent inquisition, of the state of the West India, whereof hee had received some knowledge by the instructions of his father, but increased the same by the advertisements and reports of that people. And being amongst other particulars assured, that Negros were very good marchandise in Hispaniola, and that store of Negros might easily bee had upon the coast of Guinea, resolved with himselfe to make triall thereof, and communicated that devise with his worshipfull friendes of London: namely with Sir Lionell Ducket, sir Thomas Lodge, M. Gunson his father in law, sir William Winter, M. Bromfield, and others. All which persons liked so well of his intention, that they became liberall contributors and adventurers in the action. For which purpose there were three good ships immediately provided: The one called the *Salomon* of the burthern of 120. tunne, wherein M. Hawkins himselfe went as Generall: The second the *Swallow* of 100. tunnes, wherein went for Captaine M. Thomas Hampton: and the third the *Jonas* a barke of 40. tunnes, wherein the Master supplied the Captaines roome: in which small fleete M. Hawkins tooke with him not above 100. men for feare of sicknesse and other inconveniences, whereunto men in long voyages are commonly subject.

With this companie he put off and departed from the coast of England in the moneth of October 1562, and in his course touched first at Teneriffe, where hee received friendly intertainment. From thence he passed to Sierra Leona, upon the coast of Guinea, which place by the people of the countrey is called Tagarin, where he stayed some good time, and got into his possession, partly by the sworde, and partly by other meanes, to the number of 300. Negros at the least, besides other merchandises which that countrey yeeldeth. With this praye hee sayled over the Ocean sea unto the Iland of Hispaniola, and arrived first at the port of Isabella: and there hee had reasonable utterance of his English commodities, as also of some part of his Negros, trusting the Spaniards no further, then that by his owne strength he was able still to master them. From the port of Isabella he went to Puerto de Plata, where he made like sales,

standing alwaies upon his guard: from thence also hee sayled
to Monte Christi another port on the North side of Hispaniola,
and the last place of his touching, where he had peaceable
traffique, and made vent of the whole number of his Negros:
for which he received in those 3. places by way of exchange
such quantitie of merchandise, that hee did not onely lade his
owne 3. shippes with hides, ginger, sugars, and some quantities
of pearles, but he fraighted also two other hulkes with hides and
the like commodities, which hee sent into Spaine. And thus
leaving the Iland, he returned and disemboqued, passing out
by the Ilands of the Caycos, without further entring into the
bay of Mexico, in this his first voyage to the West India. And
so with prosperous successe and much gaine to himselfe and the
aforesayde adventurers, he came home, and arrived in the
moneth of September 1563.

M. Postlewayt, The National and Private Advantages of the African Trade Considered, 1746

The most approved Judges of the commercial Interests of
these Kingdoms have ever been of Opinion, that our *West-India*
and *African Trades* are the most nationally beneficial of any we
carry on. It is also allowed on all Hands, that the Trade to
Africa is the Branch which renders our *American Colonies* and
Plantations so advantagious to *Great-Britain*; that Traffic only
affording our *Planters* a constant Supply of *Negroe-Servants* for
the Culture of their Lands in the Produce of *Sugars*, *Tobacco*,
Rice, *Rum*, *Conton*, *Fustick*, *Pimento*, and all other our Plantation-
Produce: So that the extensive Employment of our Shipping
in, to, and from *America*, the great Brood of Seamen consequent
thereupon, and the daily Bread of the most considerable Part
of our *British Manufacturers*, are owing primarily to the Labour
of *Negroes*; who, as they were the first happy Instruments of
raising our Plantations; so their Labour only can support and
preserve them, and render them still more and more profitable
to their Mother-Kingdom.

The *Negroe-Trade* therefore, and the natural Consequences

resulting from it, may be justly esteemed an inexhaustible Fund of Wealth and Naval Power to this Nation. And by the Overplus of *Negroes* above what have served our own Plantations, we have drawn likewise no inconsiderable Quantities of Treasure from the *Spaniards*, who are settled on the Continent of *America*; not only for *Negroes* furnished them from *Jamaica*, but by the late *Assiento Contract* with the Crown of *Spain*; which may probably again be revived, upon a Peace being concluded with that Kingdom.

What renders the *Negroe-Trade* still more estimable and important, is, that near Nine-tenths of those *Negroes* are paid for in *Africa* with *British Produce* and *Manufactures* only; and the Remainder with *East-India* Commodities. We send no Specie or Bullion to pay for the Products of *Africa*, but, 'tis certain, we bring from thence very large Quantities of *Gold*; and not only that but *Wax* and *Ivory*; the one serves for a foreign Export without the least Detriment to our own Product; the other is manufactured at Home, and afterwards carried to foreign Markets, to no little Advantage both to the Nation and the Traders. From which Facts, the Trade to *Africa* may very truly be said to be, as it were, all Profit to the Nation; the *direct* Trade thither affords a considerable national Ballance in our Favour, and is apparently attended with such a Series of advantagious Consequences, that no other Branch whatever of our foreign Traffic admits of.

And it may be worth Consideration, that while our Plantations depend only on Planting by *Negroe-Servants*, they will neither depopulate our own Country, become independent of her Dominion, or any way interfere with the Interests of the *British Manufacturer*, *Merchant*, or *Landed Gentleman*: Whereas were we under the Necessity of supplying our Colonies with *White-Men* instead of *Blacks*, they could not fail being in a Capacity to interfere with the Manufactures of this Nation, in Time to shake off their Dependency thereon, and prove as injurious to the *Landed*, and *Trading-Interests* as ever they have hitherto been beneficial.

Many are prepossessed against this Trade, thinking it *a barbarous, inhuman, and unlawful Traffic for a Christian Country to*

Trade in Blacks; to which I would beg leave to observe; that though the odious Appellation of *Slaves* is annexed to this Trade, it being called by some the *Slave-Trade*, yet it does not appear from the best Enquiry I have been able to make, that the State of those People is changed for the worse, by being Servants to our *British Planters* in *America*; they are certainly treated with great Lenity and Humanity: And as the Improvement of the Planter's Estates depends upon due Care being taken of their Healths and Lives, I cannot but think their Condition is much bettered to what it was in their own Country.

Besides, the *Negroe-Princes* in *Africa*, 'tis well known, are in perpetual War with each other; and since before they had this Method of disposing of their Prisoners of War to Christian Merchants, they were wont not only to be applied to inhuman Sacrifices, but to extream Torture and Barbarity, their Transplantation must certainly be a Melioration of their Condition; provided living in a civilized Christian Country, is better than living among Savages: Nay, if Life be preferable to Torment and cruel Death, their State cannot, with any Colour of Reason, be presumed to be worsted.

But I never heard it said that the Lives of *Negroes* in the Servitude of our Planters were less tolerable than those of *Colliers* and *Miners* in all *Christian* Countries. However, while our Rivals in Trade receive great national Emolument by the Labour of these People, this Objection will be of little Weight with those who have the Interest of their Country at Heart; or indeed the Welfare of the *Negroes*.

But to resume the Subject. As the present Prosperity and Splendor of the *British Colonies* have been owing to Negroe-Labour; so not only their future Advancement, but even their very Being depends upon our pursuing the same Measures in this Respect as our Competitors do.

That our Colonies are capable of very great Improvements, by the proper Application of the Labour of Blacks, has been urged by the most experienced Judges of Commerce. And if it be good Policy to purchase as little from, and sell as much to foreign Nations of our own Produce and Manufactures, 'tis certainly very unwise and impolitic in us not to encourage our Plantations to the extent they are capable of; in order to supply ourselves at least from thence with what we can't do without; and take from other Nations such Essentials only, as neither our own Country, or our Plantations will afford us.

From these Considerations it has been wisely proposed to extend the Planting of *Coffee, Cocoa, Indigo, Cochneal, Logwood, Hemp, Flax, Naval Stores,* and making of *Potash,* and variety of other Products, which those Lands admit of. Whereby, instead of being under the disadvantagious Necessity of purchasing such valuable and useful Merchandize of other Nations, we might easily become capable, not only of supplying ourselves, but exporting to others considerable Quantities of our Plantation-Produce. This would turn the ballance of Trade in our Favour, with Countries where 'tis now against us; and enable our Colonies to encrease their demand for *British* Manufactures, in Proportion to our Demand for their Produce.

But all Improvements proposed to be made in our Plantations, have always presupposed the Well-Being and Prosperity of our *African-Trade;* to the End that they might not be destitute of a constant Supply of *Negroes* for those Purposes: Without which, instead of Improvement, nothing but Distress and Poverty could ensue in all the *British* Colonies, while *France,* by wiser Measures, would render their Colonies still more opulent, and consequently a more formidable Nursery of Naval Power.

R. Norris, Memoirs of the Reign of Bossa Ahadee . . . and a short Account of the African slave trade, 1789

Since the labour of African slaves has been found necessary for the cultivation of the soil in the tropical climates of America, from the utter incapacity of white people to undergo that fatigue, every European nation possessing colonies there, has been solicitous to acquire a share in this traffic; nor have the most scrupulous of them entertained a doubt of their right to purchase, what the Africans exercised a right to dispose of.

Among the adventurers in this trade, the British possess, at present, the greatest share. It was during the government of the commonwealth, that Negroes were carried, in any numbers, to the British West Indies, and then, chiefly to Barbadoes: a few indeed were brought to Virginia, by a Dutch ship, as early as 1620; but it was the Royal African Company, that first carried on, from England, a vigorous commerce to Africa, during the reign of Charles II. We may form an opinion of the magnitude of it, in its most flourishing state, prior to the revolution in 1688, by considering that the company employed thirty ships annually, which delivered about five thousand Negroes in the West Indies. The increase of it to its present state, may be attributed to the enterprizing spirit of the merchants; to the superior address of those employed in the executive part of it; to the opulence of the manufacturers, which enables them to extend a credit to the former, beyond what can be had in any other country; and to the annual grants of parliament, for the maintenance of several forts, and factories in Africa. From these concurring circumstances, the British planters are supplied with Negroes, on more reasonable terms than their neighbours; and a large surplus is left, which is disposed of to the French and Spaniards for specie, and other valuable commodities.

The importance of this trade to Great Britain may be determined from the following considerations: it immediately employs about one hundred ships, which sail annually for Africa, with cargoes which amount nearly to a million sterling, and which are composed of the productions of the British settlements in the East and West Indies; and of British manufactures, to the value of seven hundred thousand pounds. The circuitous returns of these cargoes are computed at a million and an half. The artificers and mechanics employed at Liverpool alone, receive one hundred thousand pounds annually for labor and materials employed in equipping the ships engaged in it; and exclusive of the large sums paid for seamen's wages, the commissions and privilege of the captains and officers amount at least to fifty thousand pounds annually; which are generally realized there, and have contributed greatly to the rapid increase of that commercial town.

The African trade, connected as it is with the West Indian

commerce, and with the trade to the remaining continental colonies, and Newfoundland fishery, is of the utmost consequence to the employment of many thousands of our fellow subjects; to the naval power of Britain; and to the royal revenues; all which are conjoined by sympathetic ties. The value of three millions at least of domestic manufactures, exclusive of other merchandize, annually finds a profitable vent by means of the African and West Indian trades; and above five millions of property, arising from the labor of Negro slaves, employed in the West Indian islands, is yearly imported from thence: which contributes not less than a million and an half annually to the revenue of this kingdom. To carry on this immense traffic, and to supply these islands with lumber and provisions, from the continental colonies and Newfoundland fishery, gives constant employment to at least a thousand ships, and to above fifteen thousand mariners. To enumerate the fatal consequences that would inevitably ensue from a check given to this extensive commerce, much more the suppression of it, exceeds the present limits of this short sketch, but they shall be hinted in the sequel.

The adventurers in this trade, who have seen for near a century past, the Society for propagating Christianity, composed of the Archbishop of Canterbury, the Bishop of London, and many pious doctors of the established church, deriving, as masters, a yearly income from the labor of their Negroe slaves in the West Indies, which is appropriated to the increase of Christianity in the world, could not consider it as contrary to the spirit of the Scriptures, or to the principles of morality: nor could the adventurers regard this traffic as inconsistent with the natural rights of mankind, when they read in the statute of 9 and 10 of King William (which was made avowedly for extending the trade to Africa), "*That this trade was highly beneficial to this kingdom;*" a declaration of a king, who was the patron of liberty, and of a parliament that had vindicated the natural rights of mankind; and when they read also in the stat. of 23 Geo. II. "*That the trade to Africa is very advantageous to Great Britain, and necessary to the plantations.*" Which act was made by a whig king, and a whig parliament; who, when they dissolved the late African Company, granted a large sum of money as a compensation for their rights, in order that a trade thus necessary and advantageous, might be carried on with greater energy and success.

Encouraged by these, and various other acts of parliament, which declared the African trade to be highly beneficial to this nation, many merchants engaged their fortunes in it; nor could they imagine the *purchase* of Negroes from those states of Africa (who have the same right to dispose of them as the parliament has to inflict the pains of banishment or death) or consider the *sale* of them as illegal, when they knew that many able lawyers, learned judges, and illustrious chancellors had expressly declared this purchase and sale to be lawful; and to have transferred to the master such a property as could not be affected by local changes, or subsequent baptism: and when the adventurers know also, that in conformity to the declarations of these judges and lawyers, the statute of the 5th of his late and of the 13th of his present Majesty, subjected the Negroes in the West Indian islands, as well as the lands which they laboured, to the payment of all debts, owing either to his Majesty, or to any of his subjects; and directed these Negroes to be sold, like any other chattels, for satisfaction of such debts. In consequence of which, the five hundred thousand Negroes, now belonging to the planters in those islands, are pledged by the legislature, and by the nation, for payment of the debts that are due, either to the British merchants or manufacturers, or to the subjects of foreign princes; who, by a late act of parliament, have been encouraged and enabled to lend money to these planters, on the security of their lands, and of the labour of their Negroes.

Yet this trade, so highly beneficial to the adventurers, and important to the state; a trade sanctioned by the clergy supported by the judges, and authorized by the laws, has lately been condemned both in principle and practice. By the law and usage of parliament, the most trivial right of the most inconsiderable subject is never taken away, even for the public good itself, without a manifest necessity, and a full compensation. Yet an attempt has been made, and measures are unremittingly pursued, to deprive the British planters, merchants and manufacturers, of the advantage of this important traffic; and under a pretence of regulation, restrictions have already been proposed, which strike at its existence: but though the liberty of Negroes seems now to be the favorite idea, the liberty of Britons to pursue their lawful occupations should not be forgotten: for the principle which has raised the commerce and navigation of this country, and with them the landed interest and revenues of the kingdom, from inconsiderable beginnings to their present greatness, is the *right* which every man in it possesses, to carry on his own business, in the way most advantageous to himself and the society, without any sudden interruption in the pursuit of it; and the *consciousness* which he has, of the steady protection of the laws, in the prosecution of what has been shewn to be legal.

It has there appeared in evidence, that to *serve a particular purpose*, the mortality of the mariners, and of the Negroes, had been exaggerated beyond the bounds of probability and truth: that the African trade, so far from being destructive to the lives of British seamen, in the degree asserted, is, in fact, a nursery for training up men to that useful profession. That this trade is carried on as much to the ease and comfort of those that are the subjects of it, and also of those who conduct it, as it is possible for human ingenuity to devise. That the ships employed in it, are so peculiarly constructed for the accommodation of the Negroes, as to be unsuitable for any other trade. That the opinion, which has been industriously propagated, of these ships being unequal to the numbers which were said to be crowded in them, is groundless; as appears from survey and admeasurement of them, by an experienced naval officer appointed by government. That on the voyage from Africa to the West Indies, the Negroes are well fed, comfortably lodged, and have every possible attention paid to their health, cleanliness, and convenience. That the captain's cabbin is appropriated to the use of such as are sick; where proper care, and medical aid, are duly administered to them; and that, by an admirable regulation, the emoluments of the captains and officers, employed in this trade, are connected with, and depend upon, the health and good condition of those whom they have the charge of conveying. The mode of obtaining Negro slaves in Africa, has been demonstrated to be in a way perfectly fair, and equitable; by a barter with the natives. The crime of *kidnapping*, as it is termed, with which the traders to Africa have been reproached, proves to be extremely unfrequent: for the African committee, whose business it is to take cognizance of such an offence, and for which the law inflicts a heavy penalty, have reported, that only *one instance* of it has come before them in the course of near *forty years*. It has also been shewn, that, in consequence of this trade, many innocent lives are spared, that would otherwise be sacrificed to the superstitious rites and ceremonies of the country; many prisoners of war exempted from torture, and death: and the punishment of many crimes commuted from death in Africa to life in America; and finally, that it is the lot of most of those that are brought to the Colonies, who, generally speaking, were slaves in their own country, only to exchange a black master for a white one. That the wars which have always existed in Africa, have no connexion with the slave trade, is evident from the universality of the practice of it between communities in a savage state. The oldest writers, as *Leo*, and others, have represented the Africans as living in a continual state of war, and rapine, long before the commerce with Europeans was introduced among them; and no man of sense can doubt but the same practice would still continue, if no trade existed, and with greater frequency. Besides the motives of ambition and resentment, which the African has, in common with other nations of men, the turbulent and irascible disposition of a Negro prompts him to harrass and dispute with his neighbour, upon the most trivial provocations. Lured by the love of plunder, before he ever saw an European commodity (as the value of an article depends upon the estimation it holds in the fancy of him who covets it), the rude productions of the country, the trinkets of gold, or ivory, &c. were as much the objects of his desire formerly, as the acquisition of European manufactures can be at present. So far are the Whites from being accessary to these wars, as has been unjustly alleged; it is notorious, that the Europeans trading there, deprecate a war

C

CHAPTER 3

The Black Presence

Returning from the Guinea Coast in 1555, John Lok was the first English trader to bring a group of African slaves to England.[1] Their arrival in England heralded the beginning of black immigration. Complaints about the growing black community were heard during the reign of Elizabeth and with increasing frequency during the next two centuries. The slaves, brought to England against their will, were blamed from all sides for aggravating the distress of the English poor.

Within forty years of the first arrivals, some Africans had established themselves as free independent Englishmen, but the overwhelming majority remained slaves. The existence of both free and enslaved Africans seemed to contemporaries to exacerbate a problem which plagued the whole nation in the last years of the old Queen's reign: poverty and hunger. There were of course other, larger, foreign minority groups who consumed more food than the Negroes, but they were less readily identifiable and had in many cases the protection of being subjects of foreign states. The arbitrary decision of Elizabeth's government to round up and deport the Negroes[2] could not have been effected so easily against other nationals. The only 'protection' that the slaves had was the resistance put up by their owners. This resistance appears to have successfully prevented deportation on any significant scale.

Throughout the seventeenth century Africans were being incorporated into English society. The Courts of Charles I and Charles II, for instance, gave the employment of black servants a social respectability which people of lower social standing were swift to imitate.³ The most powerful impetus to black immigration in England, however, was not the growth of domestic slavery but the settlement of the West Indian islands, the development of the sugar economy and the expansion of the triangular trade.⁴

By the late seventeenth century black slaves were arriving in England in increasing numbers via the West Indies and America and many succeeded in gaining their freedom. By 1772 the size and nature of the free black community in London was causing contemporaries considerable alarm. The origins of this community probably lay in the coming together of small groups of manumitted and runaway slaves and the isolated free African who combined for accommodation, safety and protection. By the early eighteenth century Negroes formed a substantial minority in London and were felt to pose a threat to white employment. In 1731 the Corporation of London issued a Proclamation forbidding the employment of Negroes as apprentices in the city.⁵

The community of free Negroes in London was expanding perceptibly but it was a community for which freedom brought with it many disadvantages. The ex-slave had little training other than for domestic work, yet if he were a fugitive he would find it difficult to obtain employment as a free servant. He existed in the twilight zone of poverty, and of necessity was forced to live by begging, thieving and all the other arts in use among the London poor.⁶ The comments of Sir John Fielding, the Bow Street magistrate, illustrate the reactions of one troubled local law officer to the problems posed by the runaway slaves. Fielding attributed the Negroes' troubles to the way in which they were imported and used by their masters with little consideration of social consequences.⁷

Another commentator, Edward Long, a Jamaican planter who had been private secretary to the Lieutenant-Governor of Jamaica, emerged, after his return to England, as a powerful defender of the planter's interests. When in 1772 the Mansfield judgement weakened the control of the planters over their black English slaves, Long produced his *Candid Reflections* in which he denounced the Negro, English law and the philanthropists.[8] The Negro, Long alleged, was indolent, sexually aggressive, criminally inclined and beyond the pale of English society. Much of the case Long presented has of course to be placed in a West Indian context: Long the planter defending the planter's rights to his black property transposed into an English setting.

In the 1780's powerful voices emerged to counteract this sort of argument. The autobiography of Equiano, an African, was used by the philanthropists as part of their campaign against the planter propaganda. An extract is reproduced below to convey the mixed variety of experiences that a slave, even one as fortunate as Equiano, faced in England. Cherished as a child by several English families, converted at a young age to Christianity, differentiated by the colour of his skin and finally thrown back into bondage, Equiano's experiences were in many ways a reflection of the lives of thousands of his brothers in England.

Most Negroes, however, passed through life unrecorded. We are able to catch a few passing glimpses of them only through the medium of newspaper advertisements. The selection offered here is a small sample but it provides a wealth of information. In a few cryptic words we can see the profile of a lost individual and the attitude of white society towards him. Bought and sold like any other commodity, the Negro in eighteenth century England was dehumanised in much the same way as his brothers in the New World. Where he could, he ran away from his master to join the free black community. But once free, he was treated by white society as merely another, albeit more serious, social problem.

John Lok's Second Voyage to Guinea, 1554–1555

Among other things that chanced to them in this voyage, this is worthy to be noted, that whereas they sailed thither in seven weekes, they could return in no lesse space then twentie weekes. The cause whereof they say to be this: That about the coast of Cabo Verde the winde is ever at the East, by reason

whereof they were enforced to saile farre out of their course
into the maine Ocean, to finde the winde at the West to bring
them home. There died of our men at this last voyage about
twentie and foure, whereof many died at their returne into the
clime of the colde regions, as betweene the Islands of Azores
and England. They brought with them certaine blacke slaves,
whereof some were tall and strong men, and could wel agree
with our meates and drinkes. The colde and moyst aire doth
somewhat offend them. Yet doubtlesse men that are borne in
hot Regions may better abide colde, then men that are borne
in colde Regions may abide heate, forasmuch as vehement
heate resolveth the radicall moysture of men's bodies, as colde
constraineth and preserveth the same.

This is also to be considered as a secret worke of nature, that
throughout all Africke, under the Æquinoctial line, and neere
about the same on both sides, the regions are extreeme hote,
and the people very blacke. Whereas contrarily such regions of
the West Indies as are under the same line are very temperate,
and the people neither blacke, nor with curlde and short wooll
on their heads, as they of Africke have, but of the colour of an
Olive, with long and blacke heare on their heads: the cause of
which variety is declared in divers places in the Decades.

Royal Proclamation of 1601, Licensing Casper van Senden to Deport Negroes

Whereas the Queen's majesty, tendering the good and
welfare of her own natural subjects, greatly distressed in these
hard times of dearth, is highly discontented to understand the
great number of Negroes and blackamoors which (as she is
informed) are carried into this realm since the troubles between
her highness and the King of Spain; who are fostered and
powered here, to the great annoyance of her own liege people
that which co[vet?] the relief which these people consume, as
also for that the most of them are infidels having no understanding of Christ or his Gospel: hath given a special command-
ment that the said kind of people shall be with all speed

avoided and discharged out of this her majesty's realms; and to that end and purpose hath appointed Casper van Senden, merchant of Lubeck, for their speedy transportation, a man that hath somewhat deserved of this realm in respect that by his own labor and charge he hath relieved and brought from Spain divers of our English nation who otherwise would have perished there.

These shall therefore be to will and require you and every of you to aid and assist the said Casper van Senden or his assignees to taking such Negroes and blackamoors to be transported as aforesaid as he shall find within the realm of England; and if there shall be any person or persons which be possessed of any such blackamoors that refuse to deliver them in sort aforesaid, then we require you to call them before you and to advise and persuade them by all good means to satisfy her majesty's pleasure therein; which if they shall eftsoons willfully and obstinately refuse, we pray you to certify their names to us, to the end her majesty may take such further course therein as it shall seem best in her princely wisdom.

Proclamation by the Lord Mayor of London, September 14, 1731

It is Ordered by this Court, That for the future no *Negroes* or other *Blacks* be suffered to be bound Apprentices at any of the Companies of this City to any Freeman thereof; and that Copies of this Order be printed and sent to the Masters and Wardens of the several Companies of this City, who are required to see the same at all times hereafter duly observed.

Sir John Fielding, Penal Laws, 1768

The immense confusion that has arose in the families of merchants and other gentlemen who have estates in the West Indies from the great numbers of Negro slaves they have brought into this kingdom . . . deserves the most serious attention. Many of these gentlemen have either at a vast expense caused some of their blacks to be instructed in the necessary qualifications of a domestic servant or else have purchased them after they have been instructed; they then bring them to England as cheap servants having no right to wages; they no sooner arrive here than they put themselves on a footing with other servants, become intoxicated with liberty, grow refractory, and either by persuasion of others or from their own inclinations, begin to expect wages according to their own opinion of their merits; and as there are already a great number of black men and women who have made themselves so troublesome and dangerous to the families who brought them over as to get themselves discharged, these enter into societies and make it their business to corrupt and dissatisfy the mind of every black servant that comes to England; first, by getting them christened or married, which, they inform them, makes them free. . . . Though it has been decided otherwise by the judges. However it so far answers their purpose that it gets the mob on their side, and makes it not only difficult but dangerous . . . to recover possession of them, when once they are spirited away; and indeed, it is the less evil of the two to let them go about their business, for there is great reason to fear that those blacks who have been sent back to the Plantations . . . have been the occasion of those . . . recent insurrections in the . . . West Indies. It is a species of inhumanity to the blacks themselves, to bring them to a free country.

Edward Long, Candid Reflections, 1772

We must agree with those who have declared, that the public good of this kingdom requires that some restraint should be laid on the unnatural increase of *blacks* imported into it. At the same time it cannot be denied, but that the owners of Negroes, brought hither upon motives of absolute necessity, for want of other attendants in the voyage, have frequently endeavoured to send them back, and have as often been defeated, by the quirks of Negroe solicitors, and the extra-judicial opinions of some lawyers. The truth is, the Legislature, having never taken into consideration this claim of the planter over his slave, when brought within the realm, have not expressed any means by which he may continue the exercise of that claim. A Negroe running away from his master here is not by statute declared liable to imprisonment for any such offence. Advantaging themselves of this silence, they have always, by the advice of their solicitor, applied for a *Habeas Corpus,* and have been thereupon set at liberty of course, the judges not interesting themselves so far in favour of *private property* as to expound the statute in the manner the exposition was formerly made in respect to Villeins; that is, to *re-commit,* when the cause returned upon the writ appeared to be *a refusal to serve their master.* Hence, we perceive, one principal reason of their increase in the kingdom; which having a constant intercourse with her colonies, there must needs be frequent emigrations of planters, merchants, and others, from some or other of them, who pass into *Britain* on account of health, or of business, or to settle themselves at home; and come attended by Negroe domestics, as it is not practicable to get any others. Upon arriving in *London,* these servants soon grow acquainted with a knot of blacks, who, having eloped from their respective owners at different times, repose themselves here in ease and indolence, and endeavour to strengthen their party, by seducing as many of these strangers into the association as they can work to their purpose. Not unfrequently, they fall into the company of vicious white servants, and abandoned prostitutes of the town; and thus are quickly debauched in their morals, instructed in the science of domestic knavery, fleeced of their money, and driven to commit some theft or misdemeanour, which makes them ashamed or afraid to return to their master. But, after this desertion, they do not continue long unemployed; the same zealous friends and low pettifoggers, who drew them from their late master, find means, by the *register-offices* and other channels, to procure them a place in some family; and herein lies a capital part of the grievance. Many persons of rank and fortune entertain these fugitives on the footing of other servants, and often in preference to them, to the very great injury of the owner; who having paid a sum to the state for his Negroe, his services are as much the owner's property, and a part of his fortune, as the estate of the person harbouring him is that person's. This is a loss to the colonies, as well as to the mother country. In the colony their services might have proved beneficial to both; but in *Britain* we find them a dissolute, idle, profligate crew, retained in families more for ostentation than any *laudable* use. Several who have not been corrupted by too long a stay here, some particularly who have left wives and children behind, return very willingly; the major part of those who remain are of the most worthless sort; they care not what becomes of their foreign wife or child, but very soon intermarry here, and fix themselves for as long as they can find support; but when the prospect of an easy subsistance fails, they make no scruple to abandon their new wife and mulatto progeny to the care of the parish, and betake themselves to the colony, where they are sure, at least, of not starving. The lower class of women in *England*, are remarkably fond of the blacks, for reasons too brutal to mention; they would connect themselves with horses and asses, if the laws permitted them. By these ladies they generally have a numerous brood. Thus, in the course of a few generations more, the English blood will become so contaminated with this mixture, and from the chances, the ups and downs of life, this alloy may spread so extensively, as even to reach the middle, and then the higher orders of the people, till the whole nation resembles the *Portuguese* and *Moriscos* in complexion of skin and baseness of mind. This is a venomous and dangerous ulcer, that threatens to disperse its malignancy far and wide, until every family catches infection from it. In *France*, I am informed, no Negroe slave can be brought from the colonies to make any stay, except to be bound apprentice to some handicraft; at the expirations of the indentures, they must be returned to their proper colony; and as all such apprentices are young when first bound, and are bred up afterwards under the eye of an active, sober artificer, their morals may be preserved untainted, and other evil consequences prevented. The *French* have shewn much sagacity and great attention to the true interest of their American colonies, in this and many other regulations affecting them, not unworthy of being copied by other great trading nations. If these runaway gentry in *England* are invested with English rights in that absolute sense which most of their advocates assert, it will be no surprizing thing, if some among them should, by a fortunate ticket in the lottery, or other means, be able to purchase the legal qualification, and obtain seats in the *British parliament*. It is certain, their complexion will be no disqualification, and that a £.20,000. prize will overcome those scruples which some of our rotten boroughs might otherwise pretend against a Negroe representative. The possibility of this event, or of their becoming landholders in the kingdom, is not to be denied. Let us then consider, how far this unrestrained introduction of them among us is either politic, expedient, or useful—In the first place, they are incapable of adding anything to the general support and improvement of the kingdom; for few, if any, of them have the requisite knowledge for gaining a livelihood by industrious courses. They are neither husbandmen, manu-facturers, nor artificers. They have neither strength of constitu-tion, inclination, or skill, to perform the common drudgeries of husbandry in this climate and country. They apply themselves therefore to domestic service, in which they earn little more than their food and cloathing, except what they may happen to acquire by accident of fortune, by benevolence, or petty larcenies, at which they are remarkably acute and dextrous. They are neither so hardy, intelligent, or useful in menial employments as our white servants: One reason which weighs with some persons who retain them is, that they are glad to serve for less wages; a belly-ful and a life of sloth being their *summum bonum*. Admitting that there are only three thousand of them now in *Great Britain*, and that their diet, cloathing, washing, physic, and all other charges of maintenance, cost, one with another, £.30. *per annum*, there is £.90,000. annually expended in this kingdom for their subsistance; and there are likewise three thousand white subjects left to seek their bread in some other way, of whom no small number may be supposed, upon this exclusion from families, to fall into means of living injurious to the community, or to become chargeable to their parishes. The offspring of these Negroes, a *linsey-woolsey* race, acquire no credit to the people of *Britain,* and but little strength; for, by the inability of their father to maintain and bring them up at his own cost, they must needs grow burthensome to the public. There has never existed any complaint of a scarcity of white servants in this country; but, on the other hand, our laws for the suppression of beggars and vagabonds uniformly concur, in giving power to justices, to compel persons having no visible way of livelihood, and their children, to enter into domestic service, that they may not become public nuisances. The multiplication of Negroe domestics tends therefore, in a very signal degree, to defeat the wise and good purposes of these laws, since it excludes an equal number of poor white natives from that bread to which they are entitled by a prior claim, and turns them adrift to seek it by what other methods they can devise. . . .

The shoals of beggars, which overspread the streets in all our populous towns, cities, and even our villages, to the dishonour of this nation, the extravagant sums levied annually for support of our poor, amounting by some calculations to 2,500,000 *l.* and their amazing increase of late years, all indicate too clearly, that we are overburthened with an enormous number of very poor, distressed white subjects; who, for want of some employment suited to their ability, are thus thrown, as a rent-charge, upon the industrious class of our people. Upon enquiry among the labouring part, it will be found, that much of the poor's rate is appropriated to the maintenance of supernumerary children, who might be capable of earning a support, and ceasing to be objects of this tax, if they could gain employment in families, as domestic or menial servants. But the swarms of needy dependants continually pouring in, from the foreign states around us, together with the *renegado blacks* from our plantations, debar our own poor from access into families for their livelihood. Since then there is so much reason to complain of inundations from *France,* as well as from the extreme parts of *Great Britain* and *Ireland,* there can be no argument alledged, that will prove the expediency, policy, or utility, of encouraging the importation of Negroe domestics; and, if they are not necessary here in that capacity, for which alone they seem at all qualified, they cannot be deemed, in any view, as a needful or valuable accession to the people of *England*. The kingdom gains nothing by their residence in it; but, it is certain, loses, as well as the plantations, very considerably. It has been reckoned, that every man in the plantations gives employment to *six* at home. If these Negroes, before they quitted their colony, found employment each for *one* industrious subject in *England*, (which I believe is very short of the fact) here is a loss of employment to three thousand inhabitants at home; which, being added to the 3000 before mentioned, who are supposed excluded from domestic service by these interlopers, make the number of such unemployed white subjects *six thousand*. Moreover, the absence of a great part of these runaways must be replaced in the colony families by an equal number of other Negroes, drawn from their estates, and by this means there is a diminution caused of those hands, which, from the very nature of their former employ in works of agriculture, are the most beneficial to the commerce and manufactures of the mother country.

The Negroe advocates (whose scurrilous writings are sent abroad with no other design than to vilify the planters, and turn a worthless rabble of their clients loose in this kingdom, to it's manifest hurt and disgrace, and the discouragement of it's colonies, where a property in their service is unavoidably necessary) lament, "that if the West India owner is suffered to exercise a power of sending his Negroe out of *England*, back to the plantation, such a practice might be productive of *Villenage* here." To prevent a revival of which odious system, they would have every Negroe renegade protected against his master's claim, and permitted to nestle here. But surely, if every owner had been allowed, or required by law, to reclaim, and send back his fugitive, the revival of Villenage would have been much less probable; because, no *unfreed* Negroes would then have remained to become the subjects of it. Villenage is more likely to ensue, from this restraint put upon the re-exportation of them, and by the encouragement given to every vagabond Negroe to desert from his master's service in the colonies, and take refuge here in a life of vicious idleness. It is evidently not

the planter's fault, that the nation already begins to be em-
bronzed with the African tint.

I should have brought my argument to a period with the
last section, but for the deference I owe to the benevolent
sentiments of some moderate and well-intentioned persons,
who have reasoned after this manner: "Admitting that the
present circumstances of *Great Britain* make it absolutely necessary that she should have and maintain *American colonies*; and
granting that the soil in the hotter climates cannot be usefully
cultivated with other than Negroe labourers; what objection
can the planter have to put them precisely on the same footing
as our labourers in England? Since, if all were freed, they
might still be hired, as in *England*; and surely a voluntary
service is to be preferred before an exacted and slavish
obedience." I readily agree, that, if the consequence deduced
were practicable, no rational planter would object to this
general emancipation. But we must not too hastily frame
conclusions from what we observe in the climate and country
of *England*, and apply them to other countries and other
climates, where natural causes arise, which form invincible
obstacles to such an assimilation in practice, however plausible
the idea may be in theory. A planter would as soon expect
to hear that sugar-canes and pine-apples flourished the year
round, in open air, upon *Hounslow Heath*, as that the Negroes
when freed could be brought into the like necessity or disposition to hire themselves for plantation labour, which the
climate and soil of *England* have enforced upon its lower class
of inhabitants. But I shall enquire more largely how far a
general enfranchisement of our colony Negroes would be likely
to tend, either to the benefit of themselves, of the plantations,
or of the British trade, navigation, and commerce: the sure
consequence of such an emancipation would be, first, the total
abolition of sugar-making, and all other our West India
produce. It would be impossible to compel the Negroes, thus
enfeoffed with absolute freedom, to relish that due subordina-
tion which prevails in this kingdom over the labouring poor.
For want then of a superiority of whites to oblige them to work,
they would soon find themselves so independent, and so much

their own masters, as to renounce the controul of any laws enacted to force them. If we may judge of the uniform disposition of the Blacks already made free in our southern colonies (and this is no bad rule), not one of them would be voluntarily brought to gain a livelihood by *field labour*; because he could earn sufficient by other means to satisfy all his natural wants, with little or no fatigue. Idleness, it has been well observed, is the sure consequence of cheap and easy living; and none will labour, who have the means of idleness in their power: it is from this cause that no state ever yet made a considerable figure in commerce, where the necessaries of life could be obtained with little labour . . .

If I am suspected of having misrepresented the Negroe's appetite for sloth, let the following be offered as a very practicable and easy test of the truth of my positions: let but an act of Parliament be passed which shall place all the renegado Negroes now in *Britain* in the same condition here as our poor day-labourers are restricted to; let them be constrained to hard labour, in proportion to their strength, like them, for *fourteen pence* a day, from sun-rise to sun-set, for only one twelvemonth; and I will engage, there is not one of them, after the year's fair trial, but will most chearfully accept the alternative of being transported back to his colony, rather than continue in *Britain* upon such terms. I am induced to believe, that every dispassionate man, acquainted either with the temper of our colony Negroes, or the nature of the tropical climates and countries, will not hesitate to pronounce, that the scheme of a general emancipation is absurd, and likely to be productive of no real benefit either to the Negroes or to the nation; but, on the contrary, that it promises to entail the most incurable mischiefs upon both.

To conclude: I hope, while I am pleading the cause of the injured *planters*, I shall not be misunderstood to stand forth a champion for *slavery*. I am no stranger to the import of the word; but am satisfied in my own mind, that our colony Negroes do not feel those hardships under their servitude, which have *here* been usually and undistinguishingly attributed to that vague term. As a friend to mankind, I sincerely wish that useful class to enjoy freedom, in a *reasonable extent*; as a friend to my country, I cannot wish them set loose into that latitude of emancipation, which threatens injury to both. How far the late judicial sentence may be consistent with the spirit of *English law*, I will not take upon me to determine; sure I am, that it cannot be made compatible with the spirit of *English commerce.*

Olaudah Equiano, Autobiography, 1789

However, all my alarms began to subside when we got sight of land; and at last the ship arrived at Falmouth, after a passage of thirteen weeks. Every heart on board seemed gladdened on our reaching the shore, and none more than mine. The captain immediately went on shore, and sent on board some fresh provisions, which we wanted very much: we made good use of them, and our famine was soon turned into feasting, almost without ending. It was about the beginning of the spring 1757 when I arrived in England, and I was near twelve years of age at that time. I was very much struck with the buildings and the pavement of the streets in Falmouth; and, indeed, any object I saw filled me with new surprise. One morning, when I got upon deck, I saw it covered all over with the snow that fell over-night: as I had never seen any thing of the kind before, I thought it was salt; so I immediately ran down to the mate and desired him, as well as I could, to come and see how somebody in the night had thrown salt all over the deck. He, knowing what it was, desired me to bring some of it down to him: accordingly I took up a handful of it, which I found very cold indeed; and when I brought it to him he desired me to taste it. I did so, and I was surprised beyond measure. I then asked him what it was; he told me it was snow: but I could not in anywise understand him. He asked me if we had no such thing in my country; and I told him, No. I then asked him the use of it, and who made it; he told me a great man in the heavens, called God: but here again I was to all intents and purposes at a loss to understand him; and the more so, when a little after I saw the air filled with it, in a heavy shower, which fell down on the same day. After this I went to church; and having never been at such a place before, I was again amazed at seeing and hearing the service. I asked all I could about it; and they gave me to understand it was worshipping God, who made us and all things. I was still at a great loss, and soon got into an endless field of inquiries, as well as I was able to speak and ask about things. However, my little friend Dick used to be my best interpreter; for I could make free with him, and he always instructed me with pleasure: and from what I could understand by him of this God, and in seeing these white people did not sell one another, as we did, I was much pleased; and in this I thought they were much happier than we Africans. I was astonished at the wisdom of the white people in all things I saw; but was amazed at their not sacrificing, or making any offerings, and eating with unwashed hands, and touching the dead. I likewise could not help remarking the particular slenderness of their women, which I did not at first like; and I thought they were not so modest and shamefaced as the African women.

I had often seen my master and Dick employed in reading; and I had a great curiosity to talk to the books, as I thought they did; and so to learn how all things had a beginning: for that purpose I have often taken up a book, and have talked to it, and then put my ears to it, when alone, in hopes it would answer me; and I have been very much concerned when I found it remained silent.

My master lodged at the house of a gentleman in Falmouth, who had a fine little daughter about six or seven years of age, and she grew prodigiously fond of me; insomuch that we used to eat together, and had servants to wait on us. I was so much caressed by this family that it often reminded me of the treatment I had received from my little noble African master. After I had been here a few days, I was sent on board of the ship; but the child cried so much after me that nothing could pacify her till I was sent for again. It is ludicrous enough, that I began to fear I should be betrothed to this young lady; and when my master asked me if I would stay there with her behind him, as he was going away with the ship, which had taken in the tobacco again, I cried immediately, and said I would not leave her. At last, by stealth, one night I was sent on board the ship again; and in a little time we sailed for Guernsey, where she was in part owned by a merchant, one Nicholas Doberry. As I was now amongst a people who had not their faces scarred, like some of the African nations where I had been, I was very glad I did not let them ornament me in that manner when I was with them. When we arrived at Guernsey, my master placed me to board and lodge with one of his mates, who had a wife and family there; and some months afterwards he went to England, and left me in care of this mate, together with my friend Dick: This mate had a little daughter, aged about five or six years, with whom I used to be much delighted. I had often observed that when her mother washed her face it looked very rosy; but when she washed mine it did not look so: I therefore tried oftentimes myself if I could not by washing make my face of the same colour as my little play-mate (Mary), but it was all in vain; and I now began to be mortified at the difference in our complexions. This woman behaved to me with great kindness and attention; and taught me every thing in the same manner as she did her own child, and indeed in every respect treated me as such. . . .

However, when I went to London with my master, I had soon an opportunity of improving myself, which I gladly embraced. Shortly after my arrival, he sent me to wait upon the Miss Guerins, who had treated me with much kindness when I was there before; and they sent me to school.

While I was attending these ladies their servants told me I could not go to Heaven unless I was baptized. This made me very uneasy; for I had now some faint idea of a future state: accordingly I communicated my anxiety to the eldest Miss Guerin, with whom I was become a favourite, and pressed her to have me baptized; when to my great joy, she told me I should. She had formerly asked my master to let me be baptized, but he had refused; however she now insisted on it; and he being under some obligation to her brother complied with her request; so I was baptized in St. Margaret's church, West-

minster, in February 1759, by my present name. The clergy-
man, at the same time, gave me a book, called a Guide to the
Indians, written by the Bishop of Sodor and Man. On this
occasion Miss Guerin did me the honour to stand as godmother,
and afterwards gave me a treat. I used to attend these ladies
about the town, in which service I was extremely happy; as I
had thus many opportunities of seeing London, which I desired
of all things. . . .

[A year later.] When we arrived at Spithead the Ætna went
into Portsmouth harbour to refit, which being done, we
returned to Spithead and joined a large fleet that was thought
to be intended against the Havannah; but about that time the
king died: whether that prevented the expedition I know not;
but it caused our ship to be stationed at Cowes, in the isle of
Wight, till the beginning of the year sixty-one. Here I spent my
time very pleasantly; I was much on shore all about this
delightful island, and found the inhabitants very civil.

While I was here, I met with a trifling incident, which
surprised me agreeably. I was one day in a field belonging to
a gentleman who had a black boy about my own size; this boy
having observed me from his master's house, was transported
at the sight of one of his own countrymen, and ran to meet me
with the utmost haste. I not knowing what he was about turned
a little out of his way at first, but to no purpose: he soon came
close to me and caught hold of me in his arms as if I had been
his brother, though we had never seen each other before. After
we had talked together for some time he took me to his master's
house, where I was treated very kindly. This benevolent boy
and I were very happy in frequently seeing each other till
about the month of March 1761, when our ship had orders to
fit out again for another expedition. . . .

In pursuance of our orders we sailed from Portsmouth for the
Thames, and arrived at Deptford the 10th of December, where
we cast anchor just as it was high water. The ship was up about
half an hour, when my master ordered the barge to be manned;
and all in an instant, without having before given me the least
reason to suspect any thing of the matter, he forced me into the
barge; saying, I was going to leave him, but he would take care

I should not. I was so struck with the unexpectedness of this proceeding, that for some time I did not make a reply, only I made an offer to go for my books and chest of clothes, but he swore I should not move out of his sight; and if I did he would cut my throat, at the same time taking his hanger. I began, however, to collect myself; and, plucking up courage, I told him I was free, and he could not by law serve me so. But this only enraged him the more; and he continued to swear, and said he would soon let me know whether he would or not, and at that instant sprung himself into the barge from the ship, to the astonishment and sorrow of all on board. The tide, rather unluckily for me, had just turned downward, so that we quickly fell down the river along with it, till we came among some outward-bound West Indiamen; for he was resolved to put me on board the first vessel he could get to receive me. The boat's crew, who pulled against their will, became quite faint different times, and would have gone ashore; but he would not let them. Some of them strove then to cheer me, and told me he could not sell me, and that they would stand by me, which revived me a little; and I still entertained hopes; for as they pulled along he asked some vessels to receive me, but they could not. But, just as we had got a little below Gravesend, we came alongside of a ship which was going away the next tide for the West Indies; her name was the Charming Sally, Captain James Doran; and my master went on board and agreed with him for me; and in a little time I was sent for into the cabin. When I came there Captain Doran asked me if I knew him; I answered that I did not; 'Then,' said he 'you are now my slave.' I told him my master could not sell me to him, nor to any one else. 'Why,' said he, 'did not your master buy you?' I confessed he did. 'But I have served him,' said I, 'many years, and he has taken all my wages and prize-money, for I only got one sixpence during the war; besides this I have been baptized; and by the laws of the land no man has a right to sell me:' And I added, that I had heard a lawyer and others at different times tell my master so. They both then said that those people who told me so were not my friends; but I replied—it was very extraordinary that other people did not know the law as well as they. Upon this

Captain Doran said I talked too much English; and if I did not behave myself well, and be quiet, he had a method on board to make me. I was too well convinced of his power over me to doubt what he said; and my former sufferings in the slave-ship presenting themselves to my mind, the recollection of them made me shudder. However, before I retired I told them that as I could not get any right among men here I hoped I should hereafter in Heaven; and I immediately left the cabin, filled with resentment and sorrow. The only coat I had with me my master took away with him, and said if my prize-money had been 10,000l. he had a right to it all, and would have taken it. I had about nine guineas, which, during my long sea-faring life, I had scraped together from trifling perquisites and little ventures; and I hid it that instant, lest my master should take that from me likewise, still hoping that by some means or other I should make my escape to the shore; and indeed some of my old shipmates told me not to despair, for they would get me back again; and that, as soon as they could get their pay, they would immediately come to Portsmouth to me, where this ship was going: but, alas! all my hopes were baffled, and the hour of my deliverance was yet far off. My master, having soon concluded his bargain with the captain, came out of the cabin, and he and his people got into the boat and put off; I followed them with aching eyes as long as I could, and when they were out of sight I threw myself on the deck, while my heart was ready to burst with sorrow and anguish.

Advertisements concerning Negro slaves, 1659–1768

"A Negro boy, about nine years of age, in a gray Searge suit, his hair cut close to his head, was lost on Tuesday last, August 9, at night, in S. Nicholas Lane, London" (from *Mercurius Politicus*, August 11, 1659).

"A Black boy, twelve years of age, fit to wait on a gentleman, to be disposed of at Denis's Coffee House in Finch Lane, near the Royal Exchange" (from *The Tatler*, 1709).

"Negro 22 years—run away—middle Size, with English

stammering speech; cut on forehead; Jerusalem Arms, West Indies, 1706 on Left Arm; 1 guinea for Return, or voluntary Pardon" (from *Daily Courant*, March 1712).

"Mr Pryne, the Bristol postmaster, undertakes to pay two guineas and expenses for the recovery of Captain Stephen Courtney's negro aged about 20 having three or four marks on each temple and the same on each cheek" (from *London Gazette*, July 5, 1715).

"To be sold, a negro boy aged eleven years. Enquire at the Virginia Coffee House in Threadneedle Street" (from *Daily Journal*, September 28, 1728).

"To be sold, a Negro boy age about fourteen years old, warranted free from any distemper, and has had those fatal to that colour; has been used two years to all kinds of household work, and to wait at table; his price is £25, and would not be sold but the person he belongs to is leaving off business. Apply at the bar of George Coffee house in Chancery Lane, over the Gate" (from *London Advertiser*, 1756).

"A healthy Negro Girl aged about fifteen years; speaks English, works at her needle, washes well, does household work, and has had the smallpox" (from *Daily Ledger*, December 31, 1761).

"To be disposed of. A Negro Boy of 12 years old, extremely well made, good-natured, sensible and handy, speaks English well, and has had the small Pox. Enquire at Mr. Taylor's Barber's Shop, in Hart Lane, Covent Garden" (from *Daily Advertiser*, February 11, 1762).

"Ran away from his Master, a Negro Boy, under 5 feet high, about 16 years old, named Charles, he is very ill made, being remarkably bow legged, hollow Backed and Pot-bellied; he had when he went away a coarse dark brown Linen Frock, a Thickset Waistcoat, very dirty Leather Breeches, and on his Head an Old Velvet jockey Cap" (copied by Granville Sharp into a letter from a newspaper advertisement, *c.* 1768. From Sharp's Letter Book, Minster Library, York).

CHAPTER 4

The Free Black Voice

The works of the three Africans, Ignatius Sancho, Ottobah Cugoano and Olaudah Equiano, which are reprinted here contributed significantly towards the upsurge of abolitionist sentiment in the 1780s. The letters of Ignatius Sancho[1] were published posthumously and are therefore quite different from the works of Cugoano and Equiano both of whom wrote specifically for publication. Sancho was the best known Negro in London. He wrote a book on the theory of music and enjoyed a brief appearance on the stage. Among his friends he counted Garrick and Sterne, and Gainsborough painted his portrait. His importance lies in the frequent representations that he made on behalf of his fellow Negroes. The letter reproduced below, which led to his friendship with Sterne, is an example of the sort of campaign he conducted.

Cugoano's book,[2] written as a direct contribution to the philanthropic campaign, is particularly notable for its description of African life through the eyes of a former slave. It also conveys to the English reader the fears and aspirations felt by the growing community of free Negroes whose plight was beginning to weigh on the public conscience.

Of the three Africans, Equiano was the most influential politically. He was accepted as the spokesman for the black community in England. In his autobiography he captured for his audience the personal agony of the African thrown into slavery. The passages chosen here[3] describe his own experiences from his capture by hostile Africans to his final enslavement in the hands of the white slavers. Moving from the interior of what is now Nigeria down to the coast, Equiano registers his amazement at the sights he encounters for the first time: the changing African faces and surroundings, the Atlantic and finally the white man himself, as curious to an African as the black man had been to the first European travellers some centuries before.[4] This is one of the few first-hand accounts of the process of enslavement and stands as testimony for those whose voices have gone unrecorded.

Equiano's activities on behalf of his fellow Negroes were undertaken long before he caught the eye of the white philanthropists. He had tried, for example, to secure the freedom of John Annis, a free Negro who had been enslaved again in England in 1774. Such kidnappings, patently illegal, were evidently commonplace and gave a powerful stimulus to the growth of black co-operation. Whatever he did, the free Negro in eighteenth century London was vulnerable to the designs of anyone who cared to take advantage of him. As is suggested in the text reprinted here, his only protection lay in the strength of the black community.

Ignatius Sancho, Letter to Laurence Sterne, 1766

TO MR. STERNE.

July, 1766

REVEREND SIR,

It would be an insult on your humanity (or perhaps look like it) to apologize for the liberty I am taking.—I am one of those people whom the vulgar and illiberal call "*Negurs*."— The first part of my life was rather unlucky, as I was placed in a family who judged ignorance the best and only security for obedience.—A little reading and writing I got by unwearied application.—The latter part of my life has been—through God's blessing, truly fortunate, having spent it in the service of one of the best families in the kingdom.—My chief pleasure has been books.—Philanthropy I adore.—How very much, good Sir, am I (amongst millions) indebted to you for the character of your amiable uncle Toby!—I declare, I would walk ten

miles in the dog-days, to shake hands with the honest corporal.
—Your Sermons have touched me to the heart, and I hope
have amended it, which brings me to the point.—In your tenth
discourse, page seventy-eight, in the second volume—is this
very affecting passage:—"Consider how great a part of our
species—in all ages down to this—have been trod under the
feet of cruel and capricious tyrants, who would neither hear
their cries, nor pity their distresses.—Consider slavery—what it
is—how bitter a draught—and how many millions are made
to drink it!"—Of all my favorite authors, not one has drawn a
tear in favour of my miserable black brethren—excepting yourself, and the humane author of Sir George Ellison.—I think
you will forgive me;—I am sure you will applaud me for
beseeching you to give one half-hour's attention to slavery, as
it is at this day practised in our West Indies.—That subject,
handled in your striking manner, would ease the yoke (perhaps)
of many;—but if only of one—Gracious God!—what a feast
to a benevolent heart!—and, sure I am, you are an Epicurean
in acts of charity.—You, who are universally read, and as
universally admired—you could not fail.—Dear Sir, think in
me you behold the uplifted hands of thousands of my brother
Moors.—Grief (you pathetically observe) is eloquent;—figure
to yourself their attitudes;—hear their supplicating addresses!—
Alas!—you cannot refuse.

Ottobah Cugoano, Thoughts and Sentiments, 1787

We want many rules of civilization in Africa; but, in many
respects, we may boast of some more essential liberties than
any of the civilized nations in Europe enjoy; for the poorest
amongst us are never in distress for want, unless some general
and universal calamity happen to us. But if any nation or
society of men were to observe the laws of God, and to keep
his commandments, and walk in the way of righteousness, they
would not need to fear the heat in sultry hot climates, nor the
freezing inclemency of the cold, and the storms and hurricanes
would not hurt them at all; they might soon see blessings and

plenty in abundance showered down upon their mountains and vallies; and if his beneficence was sought after, who martials out the drops of the dew, and bids the winds to blow, and to carry the clouds on their wings to drop down their moisture and fatness on what spot soever he pleaseth, and who causeth the genial rays of the sun to warm and cherish the productions of the earth in every place according to that temperature which he sees meet; then might the temperate climes of Great-Britain be seen to vie with the rich land of Canaan of old, which is now, because of the wickedness of its inhabitants, in comparison of what it was, as only a barren desart.

Particular thanks is due to every one of that humane society of worthy and respectful gentlemen, whose liberality hath supported many of the Black poor about London. *Those that honor their Maker have mercy on the poor; and many blessings are upon the head of the just: may the fear of the Lord prolong their days, and cause their memory to be blessed, and may their number be encreased to fill their expectation with gladness*; for they have not only commiserated the poor in general, *but even those which are accounted as beasts, and imputed as vile in the sight of others.* The part that the British government has taken, to co-operate with them, has certainly a flattering and laudable appearance of doing some good; and the fitting out ships to supply a company of Black People with clothes and provisions, and to carry them to settle at Sierra Leona, in the West coast of Africa, as a free colony to Great-Britain, in a peaceable alliance with the inhabitants, has every appearance of honour, and the approbation of friends. According to the plan, humanity hath made its appearance in a more honorable way of colonization, than any Christian nation have ever done before, and may be productive of much good, if they continue to encourage and support them. But after all, there is some doubt whether their own flattering expectation in the manner as set forth to them, and the hope of their friends may not be defeated and rendered abortive; and there is some reason to fear, that they never will be settled as intended, in any permanent and peaceable way at Sierra Leona.

This prospect of settling a free colony to Great-Britain in a

peaceable alliance with the inhabitants of Africa at Sierra
Leona, has neither altogether met with the credulous approbation of the Africans here, nor yet been sought after with any
prudent and right plan by the promoters of it. Had a treaty of
agreement been first made with the inhabitants of Africa, and
the terms and nature of such a settlement fixed upon, and its
situation and boundary pointed out; then might the Africans,
and others here, have embarked with a good prospect of
enjoying happiness and prosperity themselves, and have gone
with a hope of being able to render their services, in return,
of some advantage to their friends and benefactors of Great-
Britain. But as this was not done, and as they were to be hurried
away at all events, come of them after what would; and yet,
after all, to be delayed in the ships before they were set out
from the coast, until many of them have perished with cold,
and other disorders, and several of the most intelligent among
them are dead, and others that, in all probability, would have
been most useful for them were hindered from going, by means
of some disagreeable jealousy of those who were appointed as
governors, the great prospect of doing good seems all to be
blown away. And so it appeared to some of those who are now
gone, and at last, haphazard, were obliged to go; who endeavoured in vain to get away by plunging into the water, that
they might, if possible wade ashore, as dreading the prospect
of their wretched fate, and as beholding their perilous situation,
having every prospect of difficulty and surrounding danger.

What with the death of some of the original promoters and
proposers of this charitable undertaking, and the death and
deprivation of others that were to share the benefit of it, and
by the adverse motives of those employed to be the conductors
thereof, we think it will be more than what can be well
expected, if we ever hear of any good in proportion to so great,
well-designed, laudable and expensive charity. Many more of
the Black People still in this country would have, with great
gladness, embraced the opportunity, longing to reach their
native land; but as the old saying is, A burnt child dreads the
fire, some of these unfortunate sons and daughters of Africa
have been severally unlawfully dragged away from their native

abodes, under various pretences, by the insidious treachery of others, and have been brought into the hands of barbarous robbers and pirates, and, like sheep to the market, have been sold into captivity and slavery, and thereby have been deprived of their natural liberty and property, and every connection that they held dear and valuable, and subjected to the cruel service of the hard-hearted brutes called planters. But some of them, by various services either to the public or to individuals, as more particularly in the course of last war, have gotten their liberty again in this free country. They are thankful for the respite, but afraid of being ensnared again; for the European seafaring people in general, who trade to foreign parts, have such a prejudice against Black People, that they use them more like asses than men, so that a Black Man is scarcely ever safe among them. Much assiduity was made use to perswade the Black People in general to embrace the opportunity of going with this company of transports; but the wiser sort declined from all thoughts of it, unless they could hear of some better plan taking place for their security and safety.

Olaudah Equiano, Autobiography, 1789

My father, besides many slaves, had a numerous family, of which seven lived to grow up, including myself and a sister, who was the only daughter. As I was the youngest of the sons, I became, of course, the greatest favourite with my mother, and was always with her; and she used to take particular pains to form my mind. I was trained up from my earliest years in the art of war; my daily exercise was shooting and throwing javelins; and my mother adorned me with emblems, after the manner of our greatest warriors. In this way I grew up till I was turned the age of eleven, when an end was put to my happiness in the following manner:—Generally when the grown people in the neighbourhood were gone far in the fields to labour, the children assembled together in some of the neighbours' premises to play; and commonly some of us used to get up a tree to look out for any assailant, or kidnapper, that

might come upon us; for they sometimes took those opportunities of our parents' absence to attack and carry off as many
as they could seize. One day, as I was watching at the top of a
tree in our yard, I saw one of those people come into the yard
of our next neighbour but one, to kidnap, there being many
stout young people in it. Immediately on this I gave the alarm
of the rogue, and he was surrounded by the stoutest of them,
who entangled him with cords, so that he could not escape till
some of the grown people came and secured him. But alas!
ere long it was my fate to be thus attacked, and to be carried
off, when none of the grown people were nigh. One day, when
all our people were gone out to their works as usual, and only
I and my dear sister were left to mind the house, two men and
a woman got over our walls, and in a moment seized us both,
and, without giving us time to cry out, or make resistance,
they stopped our mouths, and ran off with us into the nearest
wood. Here they tied our hands, and continued to carry us as
far as they could, till night came on, when we reached a small
house, where the robbers halted for refreshment, and spent the
night. We were then unbound, but were unable to take any
food; and, being quite overpowered by fatigue and grief, our
only relief was some sleep, which allayed our misfortune for a
short time. The next morning we left the house, and continued
travelling all the day. For a long time we had kept the woods,
but at last we came into a road which I believed I knew. I had
now some hopes of being delivered; for we had advanced but
a little way before I discovered some people at a distance, on
which I began to cry out for their assistance: but my cries
had no other effect than to make them tie me faster and stop
my mouth, and then they put me into a large sack. They also
stopped my sister's mouth, and tied her hands; and in this
manner we proceeded till we were out of the sight of these
people. When we went to rest the following night they offered
us some victuals; but we refused it; and the only comfort we
had was in being in one another's arms all that night, and
bathing each other with our tears. But alas! we were soon
deprived of even the small comfort of weeping together. The
next day proved a day of greater sorrow than I had yet

experienced; for my sister and I were then separated, while we lay clasped in each other's arms. It was in vain that we besought them not to part us; she was torn from me, and immediately carried away, while I was left in a state of distraction not to be described. I cried and grieved continually; and for several days I did not eat any thing but what they forced into my mouth.

[After a long journey to the coast] The first object which saluted my eyes when I arrived on the coast was the sea, and a slave ship, which was then riding at anchor, and waiting for its cargo. These filled me with astonishment, which was soon converted into terror when I was carried on board. I was immediately handled and tossed up to see if I were sound by some of the crew; and I was now persuaded that I had gotten into a world of bad spirits, and that they were going to kill me. Their complexions too differing so much from ours, their long hair, and the language they spoke, (which was very different from any I had ever heard) united to confirm me in this belief. Indeed such were the horrors of my views and fears at the moment, that, if ten thousand worlds had been my own, I would have freely parted with them all to have exchanged my condition with that of the meanest slave in my own country. When I looked round the ship too and saw a large furnace or copper boiling, and a multitude of black people of every description chained together, every one of their countenances expressing dejection and sorrow, I no longer doubted of my fate; and, quite overpowered with horror and anguish, I fell motionless on the deck and fainted. When I recovered a little I found some black people about me, who I believed were some of those who brought me on board, and had been receiving their pay; they talked to me in order to cheer me, but all in vain. I asked them if we were not to be eaten by those white men with horrible looks, red faces, and loose hair. They told me I was not; and one of the crew brought me a small portion of spirituous liquor in a wine glass; but, being afraid of him, I would not take it out of his hand. One of the blacks therefore took it from him and gave it to me, and I took a little down my palate, which, instead of reviving me, as they thought it would, threw me into the greatest consternation at the strange feeling it produced, having never tasted any such liquor before. Soon after this the blacks who brought me on board went off, and left me abandoned to despair. I now saw myself deprived of all chance of returning to my native country, or even the least glimpse of hope of gaining the shore, which I now considered as friendly; and I even wished for my former slavery in preference to my present situation, which was filled with horrors of every kind, still heightened by my ignorance of what I was to undergo. I was not long suffered to indulge my grief; I was soon put down under the decks, and there I received such a salutation in my nostrils as I had never experienced in my life: so that, with the loathsomeness of the stench, and crying together, I became so sick and low that I was not able to eat, nor had I the least desire to taste any thing. I now wished for the last friend, death, to relieve me; but soon, to my grief, two of the white men offered me eatables; and, on my refusing to eat, one of them held me fast by the hands, and laid me across I think the windlass, and tied my feet, while the other flogged me severely. I had never experienced any thing of this kind before; and although, not being used to the water, I naturally feared that element the first time I saw it, yet nevertheless, could I have got over the nettings, I would have jumped over the side, but I could not; and, besides, the crew used to watch us very closely who were not chained down to the decks, lest we should leap into the water: and I have seen some of these poor African prisoners most severely cut for attempting to do so, and hourly whipped for not eating. This indeed was often the case with myself. In a little time after, amongst the poor chained men, I found some of my own nation, which in a small degree gave ease to my mind. I inquired of these what was to be done with us; they gave me to understand we were to be carried to these white people's country to work for them. I then was a little revived, and thought, if it were no worse than working, my situation was not so desperate: but still I feared I should be put to death, the white people looked and acted, as I thought, in so savage a manner; for I had never seen among any people such instances of brutal cruelty; and this not only shewn towards us blacks, but also to some of the whites themselves. One white man in particular I saw, when we were permitted to be on deck, flogged so unmercifully with a large rope near the foremast, that he died in consequence of it; and they tossed him over the side as they would have done a brute. This made me fear these people the more; and I expected nothing less than to be treated in the same manner. I could not help expressing my fears and apprehensions to some of my countrymen: I asked them if these people had no country, but lived in this hollow place (the ship): they told me they did not, but came from a distant one. 'Then,' said I, 'how comes it in all our country we never heard of them?' They told me because they lived so very far off. I then asked where were their women? had they any like themselves? I was told they had: 'and why,' said I, 'do we not see them?' they answered, because they were left behind. I asked how the vessel could go? they told me they could not tell; but that there were cloths put upon the masts by the help of the ropes I saw, and then the vessel went on; and the white men had some spell or magic they put in the water when they liked in order to stop the vessel. I was exceedingly amazed at this account, and really thought they were spirits. I therefore wished much to be from amongst them, for I expected they would sacrifice me: but my wishes were vain; for we were so quartered that it was impossible for any of us to make our escape.

[Many years later] It was now early in the spring 1774. I sought for a master, and found a captain John Hughes, commander of a ship called Anglicania, fitting out in the river Thames, and bound to Smyrna in Turkey. I shipped myself with him as a steward; at the same time I recommended to him a very clever black man, John Annis, as a cook. This man was on board the ship near two months doing his duty: he had formerly lived many years with Mr. William Kirkpatrick, a gentleman of the island of St. Kitts, from whom he parted by consent, though he afterwards tried many schemes to inveigle the poor man. He had applied to many captains who traded to St. Kitts to trepan him; and when all their attempts and

schemes of kidnapping proved abortive, Mr. Kirkpatrick came
to our ship at Union Stairs on Easter Monday, April the
fourth, with two wherry boats and six men, having learned that
the man was on board; and tied, and forcibly took him away
from the ship, in the presence of the crew and the chief mate,
who had detained him after he had notice to come away. I
believe that this was a combined piece of business: but, at any
rate, it certainly reflected great disgrace on the mate and
captain also, who, although they had desired the oppressed man
to stay on board, yet he did not in the least assist to recover
him, or pay me a farthing of his wages, which was about five
pounds. I proved the only friend he had, who attempted to
regain him his liberty if possible, having known the want of
liberty myself. I sent as soon as I could to Gravesend, and got
knowledge of the ship in which he was; but unluckily she had
sailed the first tide after he was put on board. My intention was
then immediately to apprehend Mr. Kirkpatrick, who was
about setting off for Scotland; and, having obtained a *habeas
corpus* for him, and got a tipstaff to go with me to St. Paul's
church-yard, where he lived, he, suspecting something of this
kind, set a watch to look out. My being known to them
occasioned me to use the following deception: I whitened my
face, that they might not know me, and this had its desired
effect. He did not go out of his house that night, and next
morning I contrived a well plotted stratagem notwithstanding
he had a gentleman in his house to personate him. My direction
to the tipstaff, who got admittance into the house, was to
conduct him to a judge, according to the writ. When he came
there, his plea was, that he had not the body in custody, on
which he was admitted to bail. I proceeded immediately to
that philanthropist, Granville Sharp, Esq. who received me
with the utmost kindness, and gave me every instruction that
was needful on the occasion. I left him in full hope that I
should gain the unhappy man his liberty, with the warmest
sense of gratitude towards Mr. Sharp for his kindness; but,
alas! my attorney proved unfaithful; he took my money, lost
me many months employ, and did not do the least good in the
cause: and when the poor man arrived at St. Kitts, he was,

D

CHAPTER 5

Slavery and English Law

For centuries the concept of bondage had been absent from English law. With the introduction of slaves from the colonies, however, the law was faced with a social relationship from a very different kind of society.[1] The idea of 'ownership' of a living human body presented the common law with a fundamental problem. The natural legal inclination to uphold rights of property, whatever they might be, conflicted in this case with specific common law traditions, asserted in the course of many bitter struggles, of individual freedom.

A series of confusing and contradictory decisions in slave cases of the eighteenth century indicated a profound uncertainty in English law. The prevailing view, however, which received its authoritative expression in the Yorke-Talbot opinion of 1729, upheld the legality of slavery in England.[2] Despite several decisions to the contrary, this view was not upset until 1772. In that year the case of Somerset was heard before Lord Chief Justice Mansfield in the court of King's Bench.[3] It marked a watershed in English legal history.

Law reporting in the eighteenth century was a very haphazard enterprise, depending in each case upon the somewhat variable quality of the reporter. There may also have been, in the reporting of Somerset's case, a more deliberate political influence. Certainly Capel Lofft, who produced the only full contemporary report of the trial, inserted in Lord Mansfield's judgement several broad statements that Mansfield had been at pains not to make and which had in fact been made by

Somerset's counsel, Hargrave. Similarly, the brilliant attack on slavery by Hargrave, as contained in the State Trials report, was taken not from notes made during the trial but from a printed account of his speech published in revised form afterwards.[4] The essence of the decision in Somerset's case was simply that a slave could not forcibly be taken abroad by his master against his wishes and Mansfield subsequently went out of his way to underline this fact. The statement attributed to Mansfield in the report that slavery 'is so odious that nothing can be suffered to support it but positive law' was inserted by the compiler of the report some four years later.

However, for all its deficiencies, the case is included here because its historical significance and the quality of the legal argument of counsel. Although the issue being tried was a narrow one, both sides knew that whatever way the decision went it would have wide repercussions. The debate was therefore wide-ranging and exhaustive, and illustrates perfectly the logic and reasoning of the two contemporary schools of thought on the question of slavery.

Somerset's victory was, of course, a great triumph for the anti-slave lobby. Even the inaccuracies in the law reports acquired a reality of their own and assisted the cause. It should not be overlooked, however, that despite the decision in this case the taking of slaves forcibly from England continued after 1772.[5] In practice legal remedies were not usually available. Even the free Negro in England was often the subject of unlawful enslavement. So long as black slavery continued in the empire, injustice trod close behind every Negro no matter where he lived.

The Opinion of the Solicitor-General and the Attorney-General, 1729

In order to rectify a vulgar error, that slaves become free by their being in England or Ireland, or from being baptized, the Attorney and Solicitors Generals opinions were taken, which were as follows:

day for settling the form of the return to the Habeas Corpus. Accordingly on that day Sommersett appeared in the court of King's-bench, and then the following return was read:

"I, John Knowles, commander of the vessel called the Ann and Mary in the writ hereunto annexed, do most humbly certify and return to our present most serene sovereign the king; that at the time herein after-mentioned of bringing the said James Sommersett from Africa, and long before, there were, and from thence hitherto there have been, and still are great numbers of negro slaves in Africa; and that during all the time aforesaid there hath been, and still is a trade, carried on by his majesty's subjects, from Africa to his majesty's colonies or plantations of Virginia and Jamaica in America, and other colonies and plantations belonging to his majesty in America, for the necessary supplying of the aforesaid colonies and plantations with negro slaves; and that negro slaves, brought in the course of the said trade from Africa to Virginia and Jamaica aforesaid, and the said other colonies and plantations in America, by the laws of Virginia and Jamaica aforesaid and the said other colonies and plantations in America, during all the time aforesaid, have been and are saleable and sold as goods and chattel and upon the sale thereof have become and been, and are the slaves and property of the purchasers thereof, and have been, and are saleable and sold by the proprietors thereof as goods and chattels. And I do further certify and return to our said lord the king, that James Sommersett, in the said writ hereunto annexed named, is a negro, and a native of Africa; and that the said James Sommersett, long before the coming of the said writ to me, . . . was a negro slave in Africa aforesaid, and afterwards, to wit, on the same day and year last aforesaid, being such negro slave, was brought in the course of the said trade as a negro slave from Africa aforesaid to Virginia afore-said, to be there sold; and afterwards, to wit, on the 1st day of August in the year last aforesaid, the said James Sommersett, being and continuing such negro slave, was sold in Virginia aforesaid to one Charles Steuart, esq. who then was an inhabitant of Virginia aforesaid; and that the said James Sommersett thereupon then and there became, and was the negro slave and property of the said Charles Steuart, and hath not at any time since been manumitted, enfranchised, set free, or discharged; and that the same James Sommersett, so being the negro slave and property of him the said Charles Steuart, and the said Charles Steuart having occasion to transact certain affairs and business of him the said Charles Steuart in this kingdom, he the said Charles Steuart, before the coming of the said writ to me, to wit, on the first day of October in the year of our Lord 1769, departed from America aforesaid, on a voyage for this kingdom, for the purpose of transacting his aforesaid affairs and business, and with an intention to return to America, as soon as the said affairs and business of him the said Charles Steuart in this kingdom should be transacted; and afterwards, to wit, on the 10th day of November in the same year, arrived in this kingdom, to wit, in London, that is to say, in the parish of St. Mary-le-Bow in the ward of Cheap; and that the said Charles Steuart brought the said James Sommersett, his negro slave and property, along with him in the said voyage, from America aforesaid to this kingdom, as the negro slave and property of him the said Charles Steuart, to attend and serve him, during his stay and abiding in this kingdom, on the occasion aforesaid, and with an intent to carry the said James Sommersett back again into America, with him the said Charles Steuart, when the said affairs and business of the said Charles Steuart should be transacted; which said affairs and business of the said Charles Steuart are not yet transacted, and the intention of the said Charles Steuart to return to America as aforesaid hitherto hath continued, and still continues. And I do further certify to our said lord the king, that the said James Sommersett did accordingly attend and serve the said Charles Steuart in this kingdom, from the time of his said arrival, until the said James Sommersett's departing and absenting himself from the service of the said Charles Steuart herein after-mentioned, to wit, at London aforesaid in the parish and ward aforesaid; and that before the coming of this writ to me, to wit, on the first day of October in the year of our Lord 1771, at London aforesaid, to wit, in the parish and ward aforesaid, the said James Sommersett, without the consent, and against the will of the said Charles Steuart, and without any lawful authority what-soever, departed and absented himself from the service of the said Charles Steuart, and absolutely refused to return into the service of the said Charles Steuart, and serve the said Charles Steuart, during his stay and abiding in this kingdom, on the occasion aforesaid: whereupon the said Charles Steuart after-wards and before the coming of this writ to me, to wit on the 26th day of November in the year of our Lord 1771, on board the said vessel called the Ann and Mary, then and still lying in the river Thames, to wit at London aforesaid, in the parish and ward aforesaid, and then and still bound upon a voyage for Jamaica aforesaid, did deliver the said James Sommersett unto me, who then was, and yet am master and commander of the said vessel, to be by me safely and securely kept and carried and conveyed, in the said vessel, in the said voyage to Jamaica aforesaid, to be there sold as the slave and property of the said Charles Steuart; and that I did thereupon then and there, to wit at London aforesaid in the parish and ward aforesaid receive and take, and have ever since kept and detained the said James Sommersett in my care and custody, to be carried by me in the said voyage to Jamaica aforesaid, for the purpose aforesaid. And this is the cause of my taking and detaining the said James Sommersett, whose body I have now ready as by the said writ I am commanded."

ARGUMENT OF MR. HARGRAVE FOR THE NEGRO.

Though the learning and abilities of the gentlemen, with whom I am joined on this occasion, have greatly anticipated the arguments prepared by me; yet I trust, that the importance of the case will excuse me, for disclosing my ideas of it, accord-ing to the plan and order, which I originally found it conve-nient to adopt.

The case before the Court, when expressed in few words, is this. Mr. Steuart purchases a negro slave in Virginia, where by the law of the place negroes are slaves, and saleable as other property. He comes into England, and brings the negro with him. Here the negro leaves Mr. Steuart's service without his consent; and afterwards persons employed by him seize the negro, and forcibly carry him on board a ship bound to Jamaica, for the avowed purpose of transporting him to that island, and there selling him as a slave. On an application by the negro's friends, a writ of Habeas Corpus is granted; and in obedience to the writ he is produced before this court, and here sues for the restitution of his liberty.

The questions, arising on this case, do not merely concern the unfortunate person, who is the subject of it, and such as are or may be under like unhappy circumstances. They are highly interesting to the whole community, and cannot be decided, without having the most general and important consequences; without extensive influence on private happiness and public security. The right claimed by Mr. Steuart to the detention of the negro, is founded on the condition of slavery, in which he was before his master brought him into England; and if that right is here recognised, domestic slavery, with its horrid train of evils, may be lawfully imported into this country, at the discretion of every individual foreign and native. It will come not only from our own colonies, and those of other European nations; but from Poland, Russia, Spain, and Turkey, from the coast of Barbary, from the western and eastern coasts of Africa, from every part of the world where it still continues to torment and dishonour the human species. It will be transmitted to us in all its various forms, in all the gradatious of inventive cruelty: and by an universal reception of slavery, this country, so famous for public liberty, will become the chief seat of private tyranny.

Before I enter upon the enquiry into the present lawfulness of slavery in England, I think it necessary to make some general observations on slavery. I mean however always to keep in view slavery, not as it is in the relation of a subject to an absolute prince, but only as it is in the relation of the lowest species of servant to his master, in any state, whether free or otherwise in its form of government. Great confusion has ensued from discoursing on slavery, without due attention to the difference between the despotism of a sovereign over a whole people and that of one subject over another. The former is foreign to the present case; and therefore when I am describing slavery, or observing upon it, I desire to be understood as confining myself to the latter; though from the connection between the two subjects, some of my observations may perhaps be applicable to both.

Slavery always imports an obligation of perpetual service; an obligation, which only the consent of the master can dissolve.—It generally gives to the master, an arbitrary power of administering every sort of correction, however inhuman, not immediately affecting the life or limb of the slave: sometimes even these are left exposed to the arbitrary will of the master; or they are protected by fines, and other slight punishments, too inconsiderable to restrain the master's inhumanity.— It creates an incapacity of acquiring, except for the master's benefit.—It allows the master to alienate the person of the slave, in the same manner as other property.—Lastly, it descends from parent to child, with all its severe appendages.— On the most accurate comparison, there will be found nothing exaggerated in this representation of slavery. The description agrees with almost every kind of slavery, formerly or now existing; except only that remnant of the ancient slavery, which still lingers in some parts of Europe, but qualified and moderated in favour of the slave by the humane provision of modern times.

From this view of the condition of slavery, it will be easy to derive its destructive consequences.—It corrupts the morals of the master, by freeing him from those restraints with respect to his slave, so necessary for controul of the human passions, so beneficial in promoting the practice and confirming the habit of virtue.—It is dangerous to the master; because his oppression excites implacable resentment and hatred in the slave, and the extreme misery of his condition continually prompts him to risk the gratification of them, and his situation daily furnishes the opportunity.—To the slave it communicates all the afflictions of life, without leaving for him scarce any of its pleasures; and it depresses the excellence of his nature, by denying the ordinary means and motives of improvement. It is dangerous to the state, by its corruption of those citizens on whom its prosperity depends; and by admitting within it a multitude of persons, who being excluded from the common benefits of the constitution, are interested in scheming its destruction.—Hence it is, that slavery, in whatever light we view it, may be deemed a most pernicious institution: immediately so, to the unhappy person who suffers under it; finally so, to the master who triumphs in it, and to the state which allows it.

However, I must confess, that notwithstanding the force of reasons against the allowance of domestic slavery, there are civilians of great credit, who insist upon its utility; founding themselves chiefly, on the supposed increase of robbers and beggars in consequence of its disuse. This opinion is favoured by Puffendorf and Ulricus Huberus. In the dissertation on slavery prefixed to Potgiesserus on the German law 'de statu servorum,' the opinion is examined minutely and defended. To this opinion I oppose those ill consequences, which I have already represented as almost necessarily flowing from the permission of domestic slavery; the numerous testimonies against it, which are to be found in ancient and modern history; and the example of those European nations, which have suppressed the use of it, after the experience of many centuries and in the more improved state of society. In justice also to the writers just mentioned I must add, that though they contend for the advantages of domestic slavery, they do not seem to approve of it, in the form and extent in which it has generally been received, but under limitations, which would certainly render it far more tolerable. Huberus in his Eunomia Romana has a remarkable passage, in which, after recommending a mild slavery, he cautiously distinguishes it from that cruel species, the subject of commerce between Africa and America.

The great origin of slavery is captivity in war, though sometimes it has commenced by contract. It has been a question much agitated, whether either of these foundations of slavery is consistent with natural justice. It would be engaging in too large a field of enquiry, to attempt reasoning on the general lawfulness of slavery. I trust too, that the liberty, for which I am contending, doth not require such a disquisition; and am impatient to reach that part of my argument, in which I hope to prove slavery reprobated by the law of England as an inconvenient thing. . . . The truth is, that the ancient species of slavery by frequent emancipations became greatly diminished in extent; the remnant of it was considerably abated in severity; the disuse of the practice of enslaving captives taken in the wars between Christian powers assisted in preventing the future increase of domestic slavery; and in some countries of Europe, particularly England, a still more effectual method, which I shall explain hereafter, was thought of to perfect the suppression of it. Such was the expiring state of domestic slavery in Europe at the commencement of the sixteenth century, when the discovery of America and of the western and eastern coasts of Africa gave occasion to the introduction of a new species of slavery. It took its rise from the Portuguese, who, in order to supply the Spaniards with persons able to sustain the fatigue of cultivating their new possessions in America, particularly the islands, opened a trade between Africa and America for the sale of negro slaves. This disgraceful commerce in the human species is said to have begun in the year 1508, when the first importation of negro slaves was made into Hispaniola from the Portuguese settlements on the western coasts of Africa. In 1540 the emperor Charles the fifth endeavoured to stop the progress of the negro slavery, by orders that all slaves in the American isles should be made free; and they were accordingly manumitted by Lagasca the governor of the country, on condition of continuing to labour for their masters. But this attempt proved unsuccessful, and on Lagasca's return to Spain domestic slavery revived and flourished as before. The expedient of having slaves for labour in America was not long peculiar to the Spaniards; being afterwards adopted by the other Europeans, as they acquired possessions there. In consequence of this general practice, negroes are become a very considerable article in the commerce between Africa and America; and domestic slavery has taken so deep a root in most of our own American colonies, as well as in those of other nations, that there is little probability of ever seeing it generally suppressed.

Here I conclude my observations on domestic slavery in general. I have exhibited a view of its nature, of its bad tendency, of its origin, of the arguments for and against its justice, of its decline in Europe, and the introduction of a new slavery by the European nations into their American colonies. I shall now examine the attempt to obtrude this new slavery into England. And here it will be material to observe, that if on the declension of slavery in this and other countries of Europe, where it is discountenanced, no means had been devised to obstruct the admission of a new slavery, it would have been vain and fruitless to have attempted superseding the ancient species. But I hope to prove, that our ancestors at least were not so short-sighted; and that long and uninterrupted usage has established rules, as effectual to prevent the revival of slavery, as their humanity was successful in once suppressing it. I shall endeavour to shew, that the law of England never recognized any species of domestic slavery, except the ancient one of villenage now expired, and has sufficiently provided against the introduction of a new slavery under the name of villenage or any other denomination whatever. This proposition I hope to demonstrate from the following considerations.

The only slavery our law-books take the least notice of is that of a villein; by whom was meant, not the mere tenant by villein services, who might be free in his person, but the villein in blood and tenure; and as the English law has no provisions to regulate any other slavery, therefore no slavery can be lawful in England, except such as will consistently fall under the denomination of villenage.

The law of England only knows slavery by birth; it requires prescription in making title to a slave; it receives on the lord's part no testimony except such as proves the slavery to have been always in the blood and family, on the villein's part every testimony which proves the slavery to have been once out of his blood and family; it allows nothing to sustain the slavery except what shews its commencement beyond the time of memory, every thing to defeat the slavery which evinces its commencement within the time of memory. But in our American colonies and other countries slavery may be by captivity or contract as well as by birth; no prescription is requisite; nor is it necessary that slavery should be in the blood and family, and immemorial. Therefore the law of England is not applicable

to the slavery of our American colonies, or of other countries.—
If the law of England would permit the introduction of a
slavery commencing out of England, the rules it prescribes for
trying the title to a slave would be applicable to such a slavery;
but they are not so; and from thence it is evident that the
introduction of such a slavery is not permitted by the law of
England.—The law of England then excludes every slavery
not commencing in England, every slavery though commencing
there not being antient and immemorial. Villenage is the only
slavery which can possibly answer to such a description, and
that has long expired by the deaths and emancipations of all
those who were once the objects of it. Consequently there is now
no slavery which can be lawful in England, until the legislature
shall interpose its authority to make it so.

This is plain, unadorned, and direct reasoning; it wants no
aid from the colours of art, or the embellishments of language;
it is composed of necessary inferences from facts and rules of
law, which do not admit of contradiction; and I think, that it
must be vain to attempt shaking a superstructure raised on such
solid foundations.

As to the other arguments I have to adduce against the
revival of domestic slavery, I do confess that they are less
powerful, being merely presumptive. But then I must add, that
they are strong and violent presumptions; such as furnish more
certain grounds of judicial decision than are to be had in many
of the cases which become the subjects of legal controversy.

I infer that the law of England will not permit a new slavery,
from the fact of there never yet having been any slavery but
villenage, and from the actual extinction of that antient slavery.
If a new slavery could have lawfully commenced here, or lawfully have been introduced from a foreign country, is there the
most remote probability, that in the course of so many centuries
a new slavery should never have arisen? If a new race of slaves
could have been introduced under the denomination of villeins,
if a new slavery could have been from time to time engrafted on
the antient stock, would the laws of villenage have once
become obsolete for want of objects, or would not a successive
supply of slaves have continued their operation to the present

times? But notwithstanding the vast extent of our commercial connections, the fact is confessedly otherwise. The antient slavery has once expired; neither natives nor foreigners have yet succeeded in the introduction of a new slavery; and from thence the strongest presumption arises, that the law of England doth not permit such an introduction.

I insist, that the unlawfulness of introducing a new slavery into England, from our American colonies or any other country, is deducible from the rules of the English law concerning contracts of service. The law of England will not permit any man to enslave himself by contract. The utmost, which our law allows, is a contract to serve for life; and some perhaps may even doubt the validity of such a contract, there being no determined cases directly affirming its lawfulness. In the reign of Henry the 4th, there is a case of debt, brought by a servant against the master's executors, on a retainer to serve for term of life in peace and war for 100 shillings a-year; but it was held, that debt did not lie for want of a speciality; which, as was agreed, would not have been necessary in the case of a common labourer's salary, because, as the case is explained by Brooke in abridging it, the latter is bound to serve by statute. This case is the only one I can find, in which a contract to serve for life is mentioned; and even in this case, there is no judicial decision on the force of it. Nor did the nature of the case require any opinion upon such a contract; the action not being to establish the contract against the servant, but to enforce payment against the master's executors for arrears of salary in respect of service actually performed; and therefore this case will scarce bear any inference in favour of a contract to serve for life. Certain also it is, that a service for life in England is not usual, except in the case of a military person; whose service, though in effect for life, is rather so by the operation of the yearly acts for regulating the army, and of the perpetual act for governing the navy, than in consequence of any express agreement. However, I do not mean absolutely to deny the lawfulness of agreeing to serve for life; nor will the inferences I shall draw from the rules of law concerning servitude by contract, be in the least affected by admitting such agreements to be lawful. The law of England may perhaps give effect to a contract of service for life; but that is the *ne plus ultra* of servitude by contract in England. It will not allow the servant to invest the master with an arbitrary power of correcting, imprisoning, or alienating him; it will not permit him to renounce the capacity of acquiring and enjoying property, or to transmit a contract of service to his issue. In other words, it will not permit the servant to incorporate into his contract the ingredients of slavery. And why is it that the law of England rejects a contract of slavery? The only reason to be assigned is, that the law of England, acknowledging only the antient slavery which is now expired, will not allow the introduction of a new species, even though founded on consent of the party. The same reason operates with double force against a new slavery founded on captivity in war, and introduced from another country. Will the law of England condemn a new slavery commencing by consent of the party, and at the same time approve of one founded on force, and most probably on oppression also? Will the law of England invalidate a new slavery commencing in this country, when the title to the slavery may be fairly examined; and at the same time give effect to a new slavery introduced from another country, when disproof of the slavery must generally be impossible? This would be rejecting and receiving a new slavery at the same moment; rejecting slavery the least odious, receiving slavery the most odious: and by such an inconsistency, the wisdom and justice of the English law would be completely dishonoured. Nor will this reasoning be weakened by observing that our law permitted villenage, which was a slavery confessed to originate from force and captivity in war; because that was a slavery coeval with the first formation of the English constitution, and consequently had a commencement here prior to the establishment of those rules which the common law furnishes against slavery by contract.

From this examination of the several objections in favour of slavery in England, I think myself well warranted to observe, that instead of being weakened, the arguments against slavery in England have derived an additional force. The result is, not merely that negroes become free on being brought into this country, but that the law of England confers the gift of liberty entire and unincumbered; not in name only, but really and substantially; and consequently that Mr. Steuart cannot have the least right over Sommersett the negro, either in the open character of a slave, or in the disguised one of an ordinary servant.

In the outset of the argument I made a second question on Mr. Steuart's authority to enforce his right, if he has any, by transporting the negro out of England. Few words will be necessary on this point, which my duty as counsel for the negro requires me to make, in order to give him every possible chance of a discharge from his confinement, and not from any doubt of success on the question of slavery.

If in England the negro continues a slave to Mr. Steuart, he must be content to have the negro subject to those limitations which the laws of villenage imposed on the lord in the enjoyment of his property in the villein; there being no other laws to regulate slavery in this country. But even those laws did not permit that high act of dominion which Mr. Steuart has exercised; for they restrained the lord from forcing the villein out of England. The law, by which the lord's power over his villein was thus limited, has reached the present times. It is a law made in the time of the first William, and the words of it are, 'prohibemus ut nullus vendat hominem extra patriam'.

If Mr. Steuart had claimed the negro as a servant by contract, and in his return to the Habeas Corpus had stated a written agreement to leave England as Mr. Steuart should require, signed by the negro, and made after his arrival in England, when he had a capacity of contracting, it might then have been a question, whether such a contract in writing would have warranted Mr. Steuart in compelling the performance of it, by forcibly transporting the negro out of this country? I am myself satisfied, that no contract, however solemnly entered into, would have justified such violence. It is contrary to the genius of the English law, to allow any enforcement of agreements or contracts, by any other compulsion, than that from our courts of justice. The exercise of such a power is not lawful in cases of agreements for property; much less ought it to be so for enforcing agreements against the person. Besides, is it reasonable to suppose, that the law of England would permit that against the servant by contract, which is denied against the slave? Nor are great authorities wanting to acquit the law of England of such an inconsistency, and to shew, that a contract will not warrant a compulsion by imprisonment, and consequently much less by transporting the party out of this kingdom. Lord Hobart, whose extraordinary learning, judgment, and abilities, have always ranked his opinion amongst the highest authorities of law, expressly says, that the body of a freeman cannot be made subject to distress or imprisonment by contract, but only by judgment. There is, however, one case, in which it is said that the performance of a service to be done abroad, may be compelled without the intervention of a court of justice; I mean the case of an infant-apprentice, bound by proper indentures to a mariner or other person, where the nature of the service imports, that it is to be done out of the kingdom, and the party, by reason of his infancy, is liable to a coercion not justifiable in ordinary cases. The Habeas Corpus Act goes a step further; and persons who, by contract in writing, agree with a merchant or owner of a plantation, or any other person, to be transported beyond sea, and receive earnest on such agreements, are excepted from the benefit of that statute. I must say, that the exception appears very unguarded; and if the law as it was previous to this statute, did entitle the subject to the Habeas Corpus in the case which the statute excepts, it can only operate in excluding him in that particular case from the additional provisions of the statute, and cannot, I presume, be justly extended to deprive him of the Habeas Corpus, as the common law gave it before the making of the statute.

Upon the whole, the return to the Habeas Corpus in the present case, in whatever way it is considered, whether by inquiry into the foundation of Mr. Steuart's right to the person and service of the negro, or by reference to the violent manner in which it has been attempted to enforce that right, will appear equally unworthy of this court's approbation. By condemning the return, the revival of domestic slavery will be rendered as impracticable by introduction from our colonies and from other

countries, as it is by commencement here. Such a judgment will
be no less conducive to the public advantage, than it will be
conformable to natural justice, and to principles and authorities
of law; and this court, by effectually obstructing the admission
of the new slavery of negroes into England, will in these times
reflect as much honour on themselves, as the great judges, their
predecessors, formerly acquired, by contributing so uniformly
and successfully to the suppression of the old slavery of villenage.

Mr. *Dunning.*—It is incumbent on me to justify captain
Knowles's detainer of the negro; this will be effected, by
proving a right in Mr. Steuart; even a supposed one: for till
that matter was determined, it were somewhat unaccountable
that a negro should depart his service, and put the means out
of his power of trying that right to effect, by a flight out of the
kingdom. I will explain what appears to me the foundation of
Mr. Steuart's claim. Before the writ of Habeas Corpus issued
in the present case, there was, and there still is, a great number
of slaves in Africa, (from whence the American plantations are
supplied) who are saleable, and in fact sold. Under all these
descriptions is James Sommersett. Mr. Steuart brought him
over to England; purposing to return to Jamaica, the negro
chose to depart the service, and was stopt and detained by
captain Knowles, until his master should set sail and take him
away to be sold in Jamaica. The gentlemen on the other side,
to whom I impute no blame, but on the other hand much
commendation, have advanced many ingenious propositions;
part of which are undeniably true, and part (as is usual in
compositions of ingenuity) very disputable. It is my misfortune
to address an audience, the greater part of which, I fear, are
prejudiced the other way. But wishes, I am well convinced, will
never enter into your lordships' minds, to influence the determination of the point: this cause must be what in fact and law it
is; its fate, I trust, therefore, depends on fixt invariable rules,
resulting by law from the nature of the case. For myself, I
would not be understood to intimate a wish in favour of
slavery by any means; nor on the other side to be supposed the
maintainer of an opinion contrary to my own judgment. I am

bound by duty to maintain those arguments which are most useful to captain Knowles, as far as is consistent with truth; and if his conduct has been agreeable to the laws throughout, I am under a farther indispensible duty to support it. I ask no other attention than may naturally result from the importance of the question: less than this I have no reason to expect; more, I neither demand nor wish to have allowed. Many alarming apprehensions have been entertained of the consequence of the decision, either way. About 14,000 slaves, from the most exact intelligence I am able to procure, are at present here. . . . Let me take notice, neither the air of England is too pure for a slave to breathe in, nor have the laws of England rejected servitude. Villenage in this country is said to be worn out; the propriety of the expression strikes me a little. Are the laws not existing by which it was created? A matter of more curiosity than use, it is, to enquire when that set of people ceased. The statute of tenures did not however abolish villenage in gross; it left persons of that condition in the same state as before; if their descendants are all dead, the gentlemen are right to say the subject of those laws is gone, but not the law; if the subject revives, the law will lead the subject. If the statute of Charles the 2nd, ever be repealed, the law of villenage revives in its full force. If my learned brother the serjeant, or the other gentlemen who argued on the supposed subject of freedom, will go through an operation my reading assures me will be sufficient for that purpose, I shall claim them as property. I won't, I assure them, make a rigorous use of my power; I will neither sell them, eat them, nor part with them. It would be a great surprize, and some inconvenience, if a foreigner bringing over a servant, as soon as he got hither, must take care of his carriage, his horse, and himself in whatever method he might have the luck to invent. He must find his way to London on foot. He tells his servant, Do this; the servant replies, Before I do it, I think fit to inform you, Sir, the first step on this happy land sets all men on a perfect level; you are just as much obliged to obey my commands. Thus, neither superior, or inferior, both go without their dinner. We should find singular comfort, on entering the limits of a foreign country, to be thus at once devested of all attendance and all accommodation. The gentlemen have collected more reading than I have leisure to collect, or industry (I must own) if I had leisure: very laudable pains have been taken, and very ingenious, in collecting the sentiments of other countries, which I shall not much regard, as affecting the point or jurisdiction of this court. In Holland, so far from perfect freedom, (I speak from knowledge) there are, who without being conscious of contract, have for offences perpetual labour imposed, and death the condition annexed to non-performance. Either all the different ranks must be allowed natural, which is not readily conceived, or there are political ones, which cease not on change of soil. But in what manner is the negro to be treated? How far lawful to detain him? My footman, according to my agreement, is obliged to attend me from this city, or he is not; if no condition, that he shall not be obliged, from hence he is obliged, and no injury done.

A servant of a sheriff, by the command of his master, laid hand gently on another servant of his master, and brought him before his master, who himself compelled the servant to his duty; an action of assault and battery, and false imprisonment, was brought; and the principal question was, on demurrer, whether the master could command the servant, though he might have justified his taking of the servant by his own hands? The convenience of the public is far better provided for, by this private authority of the master, than if the lawfulness of the command were liable to be litigated every time a servant thought fit to be negligent or troublesome.

Is there a doubt, but a negro might interpose in the defence of a master, or a master in defence of a negro? If to all purposes of advantage, mutuality requires the rule to extend to those of disadvantage. It is said, as not formed by contract, no restraint can be placed by contract. Whichever way it was formed, the consequences, good or ill, follow from the relation, not the manner of producing it. I may observe, there is an establishment, by which magistrates compel idle or dissolute persons, of various ranks and denominations, to serve. In the case of apprentices bound out by the parish, neither the trade is left to the choice of those who are to serve, nor the consent of parties necessary; no contract therefore is made in the former instance, none in the latter; the duty remains the same. The ease of contract for life quoted from the year-books, was recognized as valid; the solemnity only of an instrument judged requisite. Your lordships, (this variety of service, with divers other sorts, existing by law here,) have the option of classing him amongst those servants which he most resembles in condition: therefore, (it seems to me) are by law authorised to enforce a service for life in the slave, that being a part of his situation before his coming hither; which, as not incompatible, but agreeing with our laws, may justly subsist here: . . .

Davy, Serj.—My learned friend has thought proper to consider the question in the opening of his speech, as of great importance; it is indeed so; but not for those reasons principally assigned by him. I apprehend, my lord, the honour of England, the honour of the laws of every Englishman, here or abroad, is now concerned. He observes, the number is 14,000 or 15,000; if so, high time to put an end to the practise; more especially since they must be sent back as slaves, though servants here. The increase of such inhabitants here, not interested in the prosperity of a country, is very pernicious; in an island, which can as such, not extend its limits nor consequently maintain more than a certain number of inhabitants, dangerous in excess. . . . Thus, foreign superfluous inhabitants augmenting perpetually, are ill to be allowed; a nation of enemies at the heart of a state, still worse.

Lord *Mansfield*.—The question is, if the owner had a right to detain the slave, for the sending of him over to be sold in Jamaica. In five or six cases of this nature, I have known it to be accommodated by agreement between the parties: on its first coming before me, I strongly recommended it here. But if the parties will have it decided, we must give our opinion. Compassion will not, on the one hand, nor inconvenience on the other, be to decide; but the law: in which the difficulty will be principally from the inconvenience on both sides. Contract for sale of a slave is good here; the sale is a matter to which the law properly and readily attaches, and will maintain the price according to the agreement. But here the person of the slave himself is immediately the object of enquiry; which makes a very material difference. The now question is, Whether any dominion, authority or coercion can be exercised in this country, on a slave according to the American laws? The difficulty of adopting the relation, without adopting it in all its consequences, is indeed extreme; and yet, many of those consequences are absolutely contrary to the muncipal law of England. We have no authority to regulate the conditions in which law shall operate. On the other hand, should we think the coercive power cannot be exercised: it is now about 50 years since the opinion given by two of the greatest men of their own or any times, (since which no contract has been brought to trial, between the masters and slaves;) the service performed by the slaves without wages, is a clear indication they did not think themselves free by coming hither. The setting 14,000 or 15,000 men at once loose by a solemn opinion, is very disagreeable in the effects it threatens. There is a case in Hobart, (Coventry and Woodfall),) where a man had contracted to go as a mariner: but the now case will not come within that decision. Mr. Steuart advances no claims on contract; he rests his whole demand on a right to the negro as slave, and mentions the purpose of detainure to be the sending of him over to be sold in Jamaica.

On the part of Sommersett the case which we gave notice should be decided this day the Court now proceeds to give its opinion. . . . We pay all due attention to the opinion of Sir Philip Yorke, and lord chancellor Talbot, whereby they pledged themselves to the British planters, for all the legal consequences of slaves coming over to this kingdom or being baptised, recognised by lord Hardwicke, sitting as chancellor on the 19th of October, 1749, that trover would lie: that a notion had prevailed, if a negro came over, or became a Christian, he was emancipated, but no ground in law: that he and lord Talbot, when attorney and soliciter-general, were of opinion, that no such claim for freedom was valid; that though

CHAPTER 6

Black Caricature

Between the mid-eighteenth century and emancipation, arguments for or against black freedom tended to focus on the personality and natural characteristics of the slave. From the extracts contained in this chapter the reader can gain an impression of the slave lobby's propaganda and the image of the Negro which it conveyed.

To some extent the ground had already been prepared. Descriptions of the African, going back to the narratives of the late medieval travel writers, had implanted in popular consciousness certain alleged 'characteristics' of the Negro. A popular caricature therefore existed, which it was in the planters' interests to promote. To this end they produced accounts of slave life which filled out and embellished the existing popular image of the Negro with 'observations' from West Africa and the West Indies.

The planters' propaganda was furthered substantially by those with personal experience of slave societies, men with West Indian properties, metropolitan influence and literary talents. Of the absentee planters living in England, one of the most influential was Edward Long (1734–1813), who had lived in Jamaica for twelve years. In 1774 Long published his *History of Jamaica*,[1] a classic description of the machinery of colonial government on the eve of the American Revolution. In a section dealing with the Negro, the traditional caricature is given greater credibility by an impressive range of scholarly references. Long was a much respected author and his opinion on the Negro, enveloped in scholarship and supported by experience and technical expertise in government, made a profound impact. He was among the most extreme in his animosity towards the slaves and, as a propagandist, the most widely read.

The career of Bryan Edwards was similar to that of his friend and associate Long. Born in England and inheriting Jamaican property, Edwards became a leading figure in the Jamaican Assembly before returning to England in 1792 to continue a successful political career. He produced his *History, civil and commercial, of the British Colonies and the West Indies*,[2] in 1793, which, like Long's became a classic planter's text. Unique as a guide to conditions in the West Indies in the last few years of the century, Edward's *History* again took the reader behind the scenes into the world of the slave as viewed by his master. Edwards had a milder attitude towards the Negro than had Long, but his portrait is nonetheless distorted. His typical slave was indolent, lying, thieving and promiscuous, without any of the talents and achievements upon which Europeans so prided themselves. The selections from Long and Edwards presented in this chapter contain the extreme form of caricature with which the philanthropists had to contend.

Thomas Carlyle (1795–1881) and Anthony Trollope (1815–1882) can be seen as the successors to Long and Edwards. Carlyle, historian, essayist, chartist and friend of Italian unity revealed himself, in 1849, to have a streak of bitterness and racialism which was to become more pronounced later. It brought an end to his friendship with John Stuart Mill when *Fraser's Magazine* published his essay, *Discourse on the Nigger Question*[3] in 1849 and Mill's answer to it in the following year.

Carlyle's essay originated in his despair at the chaos he had seen in Ireland in 1848. Instead of commenting on Ireland, however, he directed his attention towards the post-emancipation sugar colonies, now bankrupt and abandoned by the former slaves. Carlyle drew bitter comparisons between the lot of the Negroes and that of the Irish peasants, but his most ferocious attack was reserved for the school of philanthropy which, he claimed, had been responsible for the decline of the West Indies. In concentrating on the black slave, he argued, philanthropists had ignored the equally great plight of white men nearer home. Carlyle was by this time well-known and despite the refutation of his argument by Mill in the following year, the contribution made by his essay to the traditional caricature (and also to the American slave lobby) was considerable. It remains a shameful landmark in the English vituperation of the Negro.

Anthony Trollope's visit to the West Indies on postal business in 1858 resulted in *The West Indies and the Spanish Main*,[4] published in the following year. Coming almost a decade after Carlyle's contribution, Trollope's views are of interest for the continuity of bitterness and mythology, worthy of an eighteenth century planter, which they display. Prejudice was feeding on prejudice, an ever increasing weight on the minds of generations of Englishmen.

Edward Long, History of Jamaica, 1774

NEGROES.

I shall divide this people into two classes, the native, or Creole blacks, and the imported, or Africans; but, before I come to speak of those who inhabit Jamaica, I shall beg to premise some remarks upon the Negroes in general found on that part of the African continent, called Guiney, or Negroland. The particulars wherein they differ most essentially from the Whites are, first, in respect to their bodies, viz. the dark membrane which communicates that black colour to their skins, which does not alter by transportation into other climates, and which they never lose, except by such diseases, or casualties, as destroy the texture of it, for example, the leprosy, and accidents of burning or scalding. Negroes have been introduced into the North American colonies near 150 years. The winters, especially at New York and New England, are more severe than in Europe. Yet the Blacks born here, to the third and fourth generation, are not at all different in colour from those Negroes who are brought directly from Africa; whence it may be concluded very properly, that Negroes, or their posterity, do not change colour, though they continue ever so long in a cold climate.

Secondly, A covering of wool, like the bestial fleece, instead of hair.

Thirdly, The roundness of their eyes, the figure of their ears, tumid nostrils, flat noses, invariable thick lips, and general large size of the female nipples, as if adapted by nature to the peculiar conformation of their children's mouths.

Fourthly, The black colour of the lice which infest their bodies. This peculiar circumstance I do not remember to have seen noticed by any naturalist; they resemble the white lice in shape, but in general are of larger size. It is known, that there is a very great variety of these insects; and some say, that almost all animals have their peculiar sort.

Fifthly, Their bestial or fetid smell, which they all have in a greater or less degree; the Congo's, Arada's, Quaqua's, and Angola's, particularly the latter, who are likewise the most stupid of the Negroe race, are the most offensive; and those of Senegal (who are distinguished from the other herds by greater acuteness of understanding and mildness of disposition) have the least of this noxious odour.

This scent in some of them is so excessively strong, especially when their bodies are warmed either by exercise or anger, that it continues in places where they have been near a quarter of an hour.

I shall next consider their disparity, in regard to the faculties of the mind. Under this head we are to observe, that they remain at this time in the same rude situation in which they were found two thousand years ago.

In general, they are void of genius, and seem almost incapable of making any progress in civility of science. They have no plan or system of morality among them. Their barbarity to their children debases their nature even below that of brutes. They have no moral sensations; no taste but for women; gormondizing, and drinking to excess; no wish but to be idle. Their children, from their tenderest years, are suffered to deliver themselves up to all that nature suggests to them. Their houses are miserable cabbins. They conceive no pleasure from the most beautiful parts of their country, preferring the more sterile. Their roads, as they call them, are mere sheep-paths, twice as long as they need be, and almost impassable. Their country in most parts is one continued wilderness, beset with briars and thorns. They use neither carriages, nor beasts of burthen. They are represented by all authors as the vilest of the human kind, to which they have little more pretension of resemblance than what arises from their exterior form.

For the honour of human nature it were to be wished, that these descriptions could with justice be accused of exaggeration; but, in respect to the modern Africans, we find the charge corroborated, and supported by a consistent testimony of so many men of different nations, who have visited the coast, that it is difficult to believe they have all been guilty of mis-representing these people; more especially, as they tally exactly with the character of the Africans that are brought into our plantations. This brutality somewhat diminishes, when they are imported young, after they become habituated to cloathing and a regular discipline of life; but many are never reclaimed, and continue savages, in every sense of the word, to their latest period. We find them marked with the same bestial manners, stupidity, and vices, which debase their brethren on the continent, who seem to be distinguished from the rest of man-kind, not in person only, but in possessing, in abstract, every species of inherent turpitude that is to be found dispersed at large among the rest of the human creation, with scarce a single virtue to extenuate this shade of character, differing in this particular from all other men; for, in other countries, the most abandoned villain we ever heard of has rarely, if ever, been known unportioned with some one good quality at least, in his composition. It is astonishing, that, although they have been acquainted with Europeans, and their manufactures, for so many hundred years, they have, in all this series of time, manifested so little taste for arts, or a genius either inventive or imitative. Among so great a number of provinces on this extensive continent, and among so many millions of people, we have heard but of one or two insignificant tribes, who comprehend any thing of mechanic arts, or manufacture; and even these, for the most part, are said to perform their work in a very bungling and slovenly manner, perhaps not better than an *oran-outang* might, with a little pains, be brought to do.

The Negroes seem to conform nearest in character to the Ægyptians, in whose government, says the learned Goguet, there reigned a multitude of abuses, and essential defects, authorized by the laws, and by their fundamental principles. As to their customs and manners, indecency and debauchery were carried to the most extravagant height, in all their public feasts, and religious ceremonies; neither was their morality pure. It offended against the first rules of rectitude and probity; they lay under the highest censure for covetousness, perfidy, cunning, and roguery. They were a people without taste, without genius, or discernment; who had only ideas of grandeur, ill understood: knavish, crafty, soft, lazy, cowardly, and servile, superstitious in excess, and extravagantly besotted with an absurd and monstrous theology; without any skill in eloquence, poetry, music, architecture, sculpture, or painting, navigation, commerce, or the art military. Their intellect rising to but a very confused notion, and imperfect idea, of the general objects of human knowledge. But he allows, that they invented some arts, and some sciences; that they had some little knowledge of astronomy, geography, and the mathematics; that they had some few good civil laws and political constitutions; were industrious enough adepts in judicial astrology; though their skill in sculpture, and architecture, rose not above a flat mediocrity. In these acquisitions, however imperfect, they appear far superior to the Negroes, who, perhaps, in their turn, as far transcend the Ægyptians in the superlative perfection of their worst qualities.

When we reflect on the nature of these men, and their dissimilarity to the rest of mankind, must we not conclude, that they are a different species of the same *genus?*

(After describing various kinds of animals, Long continues) ... from these we come to the *oran-outang* species, who have some trivial resemblance to the ape-kind, but the strongest similitude to mankind, in countenance, figure, statute, organs, erect posture, actions or movements, food, temper, and manner of living.

The oran-outangs are said to make a kind of huts, composed of boughs interlaced, which serve to guard them from the too great heat of the sun.

It is also averred, that they sometimes endeavour to surprise and carry off Negroe women into their woody retreats, in order to enjoy them.

The essential differences between the body of the oran-outang and that of a man, are reduced by Mr. Buffon to two, namely, the conformation of the *os ilium*, and that of the feet; the bone of the *ilium* is more close or contracted than in man. He has calves, and fleshy posteriors, which indicate that he is destined to walk erect; but his toes are very long, and the heel pressed with difficulty to the ground: he runs with more ease than he can walk, and requires artificial heels, more elevated than those of shoes in general, to enable him to walk without inconvenience for any length of time. These are the only parts in which he bears more resemblance to the ape kind than to man; but when he is compared with the ape, baboon, or monkey, he is found to have far more conformity to man than to those animals. The Indians are therefore excusable for associating him with the human race, under the appellation of oran-outang, or *wild man*, since he resembles man much more than he does the ape, or any other animal. All the parts of his head, limbs, and body, external and internal, are so perfectly like the human, that we cannot (says he) collate them together, without being amazed at a conformation so parallel, and an organization so exactly the same, although *not resulting to the same effects*. The tongue, for example, and all the organs of speech are the same in both, and yet the oran-outang *does not speak*; the brain is absolutely the same in texture, disposition, and proportion, and yet *he does not think*; an evident proof this, that mere matter alone, though perfectly organized, cannot produce thought, nor speech, the index of thought, unless it be animated with *a superior principle*.

His imitation and mimickry of human gestures and movements, which come so near in semblance to the result of thought, set him at a great distance from brute animals, and in a close affinity to man. If the essence of his nature consists entirely in the form and organization of the body, he comes nearer to man than any other creature, and may be placed in the second class of animal beings.

If he is a creature *sui generis*, he fills up the space between mankind and the ape, as this and the monkey tribe supply the interval that is between the oran-outang and quadrupeds. . .

The conformation of their limbs denotes beyond all controversy that they are destined to an erect position of body, and to move like men. The structure of their teeth, their organs of secretion, digestion &c. all the same as the human, prove them entitled to subsist on the same aliments as man. The organs of generation being alike they propagate their species, and their females suckle their young, in the same manner.

Their disposition shews a great degree of social feeling; they seem to have a sense of shame, and a share of sensibility, as may be inferred from the preceding relations; nay, some trace of reason appears in that young one, which (according to Le Brosse) made signs expressive of his idea that "bleeding in the arm had been remedial to his disorder." Nor must we omit the expression of their grief by shedding tears, and other passions, by modes entirely resembling the human. Ludicrous as the opinion may seem, I do not think that an oran-outang husband would be any dishonour to an Hottentot female for what are these Hottentots?—They are, say the most credible writers, a people certainly very stupid, and very brutal. In many respects they are more like beasts than men; their complexion is dark, they are short and thick-set; their noses flat, like those of a Dutch dog; their lips very thick and big; their teeth exceedingly white, but very long, and ill set, some of them sticking out of their mouths like boars tusks; their hair black, and curled like wool; they are very nimble, and run with a speed that is almost incredible; they are very disagreeable in their persons, and, in short, taking all things together, one of the meanest nations on the face of the earth.

Has the Hottentot, from this portrait, a more manly figure than the oran-outang? I suspect that he owes, like the oran-outang, the celerity of his speed to the particular conformation of his foot; this, by the way, is only my conjecture, for he has not as yet undergone anatomical investigation. That the oran-outang and some races of black men are very nearly allied, is, I think, more than probable; Mr. Buffon supports his deductions, tending to the contrary, by no decisive proofs.

(About the oran-outang) For my own part, I conceive that probability favours the opinion, that human organs were not given him for nothing: that this race have some language by which their meaning is communicated; whether it resembles the gabbling of turkies like that of the Hottentots, or the hissing of serpents, is of very little consequence, so long as it is intelligible among themselves: nor, for what hitherto appears, do they seem at all inferior in the intellectual faculties to many of the Negroe race; with some of whom, it is credible that they have the most intimate connexion and consanguinity. The amorous intercourse between them may be frequent; the Negroes themselves bear testimony that such intercourses actually happen; and it is certain, that both races agree perfectly well in lasciviousness of disposition.

But if we admit with Mr. Buffon, that with all this analogy of organization, the oran-outang's brain is a senseless *icon* of the human; that it is meer matter, unanimated with a thinking principle, in any, or at least in a very minute and imperfect degree, we must then infer the strongest conclusion to establish our belief of a natural diversity of the human intellect, in general, *ab origine*; an oran-outang, in this case, is a human being, *quoad* his form and organs; but of an inferior species, *quoad* his intellect; he has in form a much nearer resemblance to the Negroe race, than the latter bear to white men; the supposition then is well founded, that the brain, and intellectual organs, so far as they are dependent upon meer matter, though similar in texture and modification to those of other men, may in some of the Negroe race be so constituted, as *not to result to the same effects*; for we cannot but allow, that the Deity might, if it was his pleasure, diversify his works in this manner, and either withhold the *superior principle* entirely, or in part only, or infuse it into the different classes and races of human creatures, in such portions, as to form the same gradual climax

E

towards perfection in this human system, which is so evidently designed in every other.

If such has been the intention of the Almighty, we are then perhaps to regard the oran-outang as,

..   "—the lag of human kind,
   Nearest to brutes, by God design'd."

The Negroe race (consisting of varieties) will then appear rising progressively in the scale of intellect, the further they mount above the oran-outang and brute creation. The system of man will seem more consistent, and the measure of it more compleat, and analogous to the harmony and order that are visible in every other line of the world's stupendous fabric. Nor is this conclusion degrading to human nature, while it tends to exalt our idea of the infinite perfections of the Deity; for how vast is the distance between inert matter, and matter endued with thought and reason! The series and progression from a lump of dirt to a perfect human being is amazingly extensive; nor less so, perhaps, the interval between the latter and the most perfect angelic being, and between this being and the Deity himself. Let us shake off those clouds with which prejudice endeavours to invelope the understanding; and, exerting that freedom of thought which the Best of Beings has granted to us, let us take a noon-tide view of the human *genus*; and shall we say, that it is totally different from, and less perfect than, every other system of animal beings? The species of every other *genus* have their certain mark and distinction, their varieties, and subordinate classes: and why should the race of mankind be singularly indiscriminate?

  "—In the catalogue they go for *men*,
As hounds and greyhounds, mongrels, spaniels, curs,
Shocks, water-rugs, and demi-wolves, are 'clep'd
All by the *name of dogs*; the valued file
Distinguishes the swift, the slow, the subtle,
The housekeeper, the hunter; every one
According to the gift, which bounteous nature
Hath in him clos'd; whereby he does receive
Particular addition, from the bill
That writes them all alike;—*And so of men*—"

says that faithful observer of nature, our immortal Shakespeare;
and with him so far agrees that truly learned and sagacious
naturalist Mons. Buffon, who investigates the marks of variation
among mankind in the following manner: "Men differ from
white to black, from compound to simple, by the height of
stature, size, activity, strength, and other bodily characteristics;
and from the genius to the dolt, from the greatest to the least,
by the measure of intellect." That there are some physical distinctions, in respect of person, I think, requires no further
demonstration; and that men vary still more in intellect, is
almost equally evident.

(After describing various 'tribes' in Africa) Having now
compleated this tour, we are struck with one very pertinent
remark; the natives of the whole tract, comprised under the
name of Negro-land, are all black, and have wool instead of
hair; whereas the people in the most torrid regions of Libya
and America, who have the sun vertical over them, have
neither the same tincture of skin, nor woolly covering. As we
recede from Negro-land, this blackness gradually decreases,
and the wool as gradually changes to lank hair, which at first
is of a short staple, but is found longer, the further we advance.
We observe the like gradations of the intellectual faculty, from
the first rudiments perceived in the monkey kind, to the more
advanced stages of it in apes, in the *oran-outang*, that type of
man, and the Guiney Negroe; and ascending from the varieties
of this class to the lighter casts, until we mark its utmost limit
of perfection in the pure White. Let us not then doubt, but
that every member of the creation is wisely fitted and adapted
to the certain uses, and confined within the certain bounds, to
which it was ordained by the Divine Fabricator. The measure
of the several orders and varieties of these Blacks may be as
compleat as that of any other race of mortals; filling up that
space, or degree, beyond which they are not destined to pass;
and discriminating them from the rest of men, not in *kind*, but
in *species*.

The examples which have been given of Negroes born and
trained up in other climates, detract not from that general idea
of narrow, humble intellect, which we affix to the inhabitants

of Guiney. We have seen *learned horses, learned* and even *talking dogs,* in England; who, by dint of much pains and tuition, were brought to exhibit the signs of a capacity far exceeding what is ordinarily allowed to be possessed by those animals. The experiment has not been fully tried with the *oran-outangs*; yet, from what has hitherto been proved, this race of beings may, for aught we know to the contrary, possess a share of intellect, which, by due cultivation, might raise them to a nearer apparent equality with the human, and make them even excel the inhabitants of *Quaque, Angola,* and *Whidah.* Mr. *Hume* presumes, from his observations upon the native Africans, to conclude, that they are inferior to the rest of the species, and utterly incapable of all the higher attainments of the human mind. Mr. *Beattie,* upon the principle of philanthropy, combats this opinion; but he is unfortunate in producing no demonstration to prove, that it is either lightly taken up, or inconsistent with experience. He likewise makes no scruple to confound the Negroes and Mexican Indians together, and to deduce conclusions from the ingenuity of the latter, to shew the probable ingenuity of the former. We might reasonably suppose, that the commerce maintained with the Europeans for above two centuries, and the great variety of fabrics and things manufactured, which have been introduced among the Guiney Negroes for such a length of time, might have wrought some effect towards polishing their manners, and exciting in them at least a degree of imitative industry; but it is really astonishing to find, that these causes have not operated to their civilization; they are at this day, if any credit can be given to the most modern accounts, but little divested of their primitive brutality; we cannot pronounce them insusceptible of civilization, since even apes have been taught to eat, drink, repose, and dress like men; but of all the human species hitherto discovered, their natural baseness of mind seems to afford least hope of their being (except by miraculous interposition of the divine Providence) so far refined as to *think,* as well as act like *perfect men.*

It has been said, that the nature of their governments is unfavourable to genius, because they tolerate slavery; but genius is *manifested* in the right frame of government: they have republics among them as well as monarchies, but neither have yet been known productive of civility, of arts, or sciences. Their genius (if it can be so called) consists alone in trick and cunning, enabling them, like monkies and apes, to be thievish and mischievous, with a peculiar dexterity. They seem unable to combine ideas, or pursue a chain of reasoning; they have no mode of forming calculations, or of recording events to posterity, or of communicating thoughts and observations by marks, characters, or delineation; or by that method so common to most other countries in their rude and primitive ages, by little poems or songs: we find this practice existed formerly among the Ægyptians, Phœnicians, Arabians, Mexicans, and many others. The ancient inhabitants of Brazil, Peru, Virginia, St. Domingo, and Canada, preserved, in poems of this kind, such events as they thought worthy of the knowledge of future times, and sung them at their public festivals and solemnities. Arithmetick, astronomy, geometry, and mechanicks, were, in other societies of men, among the first sciences to which they applied themselves. The origin of arts and sciences in other countries has been ascribed to their uniting in societies, instead of leading a gregarious life; their necessities, the institution of laws and government, and the leisure which these afforded for indulging in such researches. It may be said, that the Negroes are not affected by this necessity which has affected other people; that their soil is wonderfully productive; that their country abounds with food; that the warmth of their climate makes cloathing superfluous; but no such pretences restrained the South Americans, and others living under the same parallel of climate, from cloathing themselves.

The art of making garments was invented in the mildest climates, where there was the least need of any covering for the body; necessity alone therefore could not be the cause of mens cloathing themselves.

The Negroes live in societies; some of their towns (as they are called) are even said to be very extensive; and if a life of idleness implies leisure, they enjoy enough of it. In regard to their laws and government, these may, with them, be more properly ranged under the title of customs and manners; they have no regulations dictated by foresight: they are the simple result of a revengeful selfish spirit, put in motion by the crimes that prevail among them; consequently their edicts are mostly vindictive, and death or slavery the almost only modes of punishment; they seem to have no polity, nor any comprehension of the use of civil institutions. Their punishments are actuated either by a motive of revenge or of avarice; they have none to balance the allurements of pleasure, nor the strength of the passions, nor to operate as incitements to industry and worthy actions. In many of their provinces they are often reduced to the utmost straights for want of corn, of which they might enjoy the greatest abundance, if they were but animated with the smallest portion of industry. If no rules of civil polity exist among them, does it not betray an egregious want of common sense, that no such rules have been formed? If it be true, that in other countries mankind have cultivated some arts, through the impulse of the necessities under which they laboured, what origin shall we give to those contrivances and arts, which have sprung up after those necessities were provided for? These are surely no other than the result of innate vigour and energy of the mind, inquisitive, inventive, and hurrying on with a divine enthusiasm to new attainments. The jurisprudence, the customs and manners of the Negroes, seem perfectly suited to the measure of their narrow intellect. Laws have justly been regarded as the master-piece of human genius: what then are we to think of those societies of men, who either have none, or such only as are irrational and ridiculous?

Religion and Religious Opinions among the Negroes.

They are said to have as many religions almost as they have deities, and these are innumerable; but some have been taught to believe the existence of a supreme God. These say that God is partial to the Whites, and treats them as his own children, but takes pleasure in afflicting the Blacks with a thousand evils; that they are indebted to him for nothing but showers, without which the earth would not afford them provisions; but even in this, they alledge he is only the undesigning cause, and for the effect they are obliged to the fertility of the soil. Man's creation they assert to have happened in the following manner: in the beginning, black as well as white men were created; nay, if there was any difference in time, the Blacks had the priority. To these, two sorts of favours were presented; to the Blacks, gold; and to the Whites, the knowledge of arts and sciences. It was from choice, that the Blacks had gold for their share: and, to punish their avarice, it was decreed they should ever be slaves to the white men; they are fully persuadedthat no country but Afric produces gold, and that Blacks can never attain the knowledge of letters.

Of some Customs among them.

In hot climates, bathing is one of the highest luxuries; it is no wonder then that we find their inhabitants universally adopt this agreeable practice, especially as cattle, wild beasts, and other quadruped animals, use it for their refreshment. The Negroes teach their children to swim at a very tender age; hence they become expert divers, and are able to continue an incredible length of time under water; hence too they incline to fix their dwellings on the sea coast, or the banks of the rivers, to save themselves the trouble of a long walk.

In these climates the brute creation fly to shelter from the rain; the Negroes likewise avoid it with extreme anxiety; if they are catched in a shower they clasp their arms over their heads to defend them, run with all the speed they can to the nearest retreat, and seem to groan at every drop that falls upon them; to preserve their bodies the better from it, they rub them over with palm oil, as the aquatic birds besmear their plumage with the oily liquor expressed from the glands which nature has provided them with. Their women are delivered with little or no labour; they have therefore no more occasion for midwives, than the female oran-outang, or any other wild animal. A woman brings forth her child in a quarter of an hour, goes the same day to the sea, and washes herself. Some have even been known to bring forth twins without a shriek, or a scream; and it is seldom they are confined above two, or, at most, three days.

Immediately before her labour she is conducted to the sea side or a river, followed by a number of little children, who throw all manner of ordure and excrement at her in the way, after which she is washed with great care. Without this cleanly ceremony, the Negroes are persuaded that either the mother, the child, or one of the parents, will die during the period of lying-in. Thus they seem exempted from the curse inflicted upon Eve and her daughters, "I will greatly multiply thy sorrow; in sorrow shalt thou bring forth children."

(On the diet of the Negro) They are most brutal in their manners and uncleanly in their diet, eating flesh almost raw by choice, though intolerably putrid and full of meggots. Even those that inhabit the sea coast, though well provided with other victuals, are so ravenous that they will devour the raw guts of animals. The unhealthiness of some of the European factories here, has been imputed in great measure to the abominable custom of the natives, of exposing their fish to the sun till they become sufficiently stinking, fly-blown, and rotten. This causes a stench, which fills all the atmosphere in the neighbourhood, and, though insupportably offensive to the Europeans, it does not seem to affect the Blacks with any other than the most delicious sensations.

At their meals they tear the meat with their talons, and chuck it by handfulls down their throats with all the voracity of wild beasts; at their politest entertainments they thrust their hands all together into the dish, sometimes returning into it what they have been chewing. They use neither table-cloths, knives, forks, plates, nor trenchers, and generally squat down upon the bare earth to their repast.

Their hospitality is the result of self-love; they entertain strangers only in hopes of extracting some service or profit from them; and in regard to others, the hospitality is reciprocal; by receiving them into their huts, they acquire a right of being received into theirs in turn. This in fact is a species of generosity which gives no decisive evidence of goodness of heart, or rectitude of manners, except in those countries where no advantage is expected to be made by the host.

In short, their corporeal sensations are in general of the

grossest frame; their sight is acute, but not correct; they will rarely miss a standing object, but they have no notion of shooting birds on the wing, nor can they project a straight line, nor lay any substance square with another. Their hearing is remarkably quick; their faculties of smell and taste are truly bestial, nor less so their commerce with the other sex; in these acts they are libidinous and shameless as monkies, or baboons. The equally hot temperament of their women has given probability to the charge of their admitting these animals frequently to their embrace. An example of this intercourse once happened, I think, in England; and if lust can prompt to such excesses in that Northern region, and in despight of all the checks which national politeness and refined sentiments impose, how freely may it not operate in the more genial soil of Afric, that parent of every thing that is monstrous in nature, where these creatures are frequent and familiar; where the passions rage without any controul; and the retired wilderness presents opportunity to gratify them without fear of detection!

Bryan Edwards, History of the British colonies in the West Indies, 1793

Thus, notwithstanding what has been related of the firmness and courage of the natives of the Gold Coast, it is certain that the Negroes in general in our islands (such of them at least as have been any length of time in a state of servitude) are of a distrustful and cowardly disposition. So degrading is the nature of slavery, that fortitude of mind is lost as free agency is restrained. To the same cause probably must be imputed their propensity to conceal, or violate the truth; which is so general, that I think the vice of falsehood is one of the most prominent features in their character. If a Negro is asked even an indifferent question by his master, he seldom gives an immediate reply; but, affecting not to understand what is said, compels a repetition of the question, that he may have time to consider, not what is the true answer, but, what is the most politick one for him to give. The proneness observable in many of them to the vice of theft, has already been noticed; and I am afraid that evil communication makes it almost general.

It is no easy matter, I confess, to discriminate those circumstances which are the result of proximate causes, from those which are the effects of national customs and early habits in savage life; but I am afraid that cowardice and dissimulation have been the properties of slavery in all ages, and will continue to be so, to the end of the world. It is a situation that necessarily suppresses many of the best affections of the human heart.—If it calls forth any latent virtues, they are those of sympathy and compassion towards persons in the same condition of life; and accordingly we find that the Negroes in general are strongly attached to their countrymen, but above all, to such of their companions as came in the same ship with them from Africa. This is a striking circumstance: the term *shipmate* is understood among them as signifying a relationship of the most endearing nature; perhaps as recalling the time when the sufferers were cut off together from their common country and kindred, and awakening reciprocal sympathy, from the remembrance of mutual affliction.

But their benevolence, with a very few exceptions, extends no further. The softer virtues are seldom found in the bosom of the enslaved African. Give him sufficient authority, and he becomes the most remorseless of tyrants. Of all the degrees of wretchedness endured by the sons of men, the greatest, assuredly, is the misery which is felt by those who are unhappily doomed to be the Slaves of Slaves; a most unnatural relation, which sometimes takes place in the sugar plantations; as for instance, when it is found necessary to instruct young Negroes in certain trades or handicraft employments. In those cases it is usual to place them in a sort of apprenticeship to such of the old Negroes as are competent to give them instruction; but the harshness with which these people enforce their authority, is extreme; and it serves in some degree to lessen the indignation which a good mind necessarily feels at the abuses of power by the Whites, to observe that the Negroes themselves, when invested with command, give full play to their revengeful passions; and exercise all the wantonness of cruelty without restraint or remorse.

The same observation may be made concerning their conduct towards the inferior animal creation. Their treatment of cattle under their direction is brutal beyond belief. Even the useful and social qualities of the dog secure to him no kind usage from an African master. Although there is scarce a Negro that is not attended by one, they seem to maintain these poor animals solely for the purpose of having an object whereon to exercise their caprice and cruelty. And, by the way, it is a singular circumstance, and not the less true for being somewhat ludicrous, that the animal itself, when the property of a Negro, betrays at first sight to whom he belongs; for, losing his playful propensities, he seems to feel the inferiority of his condition, and actually crouches before such of his own species, as are used to better company. With the manners, he acquires also the cowardly, thievish, and sullen disposition of his African tyrant.

But, notwithstanding what has been related of the selfish and unrelenting temper of the enslaved Africans, they are said to be highly susceptible of the passion of love. It has even been supposed that they are more subject to, and sensible of, its impression, than the natives of colder climates. "The Negro (says Dr. Robertson) glows with all the warmth of desire natural to his climate." "The tender passion (says another writer) is the most ardent one in the breast of the enslaved African.—It is the only source of his joys, and his only solace in affliction." Monsieur de Chanvalon (the historian of Martinico) expatiates on the same idea with great eloquence.— "Love, says he, the child of nature, to whom she entrusts her own preservation; whose progress no difficulties can retard, and who triumphs even in chains; that principle of life, as necessary to the harmony of the universe, as the air which we breathe, inspires and invigorates all the thoughts and purposes of the Negro, and lightens the yoke of his slavery. No perils can abate, nor impending punishments restrain, the ardour of his passion.—He leaves his master's habitation, and traversing the wilderness by night, disregarding it noxious inhabitants, seeks a refuge from his sorrows, in the bosom of his faithful and affectionate mistress."

All this however is the language of poetry and the visions of romance. The poor Negro has no leisure in a state of slavery to indulge a passion, which, however descended, is nourished by idleness. If by love, is meant that tender attachment to one individual object, which, in civilised life, is desire heightened by sentiment, and refined by delicacy, I doubt if it ever found a place in an African bosom.—The Negroes in the West Indies, both men and women, would consider it as the greatest exertion of tyranny, and the most cruel of all hardships, to be compelled to confine themselves to a single connection with the other sex; and I am persuaded that any attempt to restrain their present licentious and dissolute manners, by introducing the marriage ceremony among them, as is strenuously recommended by many persons in Great Britain, would be utterly impracticable to any good purpose. Perhaps it may be thought that the Negroes are not altogether reduced to so deplorable a state of slavery, as is commonly represented, when it is known that they boldly claim and exercise a right of disposing of themselves in this respect, according to their own will and pleasure, without any controul from their masters.

That passion therefore to which (dignified by the name of Love) is ascribed the power of softening all the miseries of slavery, is mere animal desire, implanted by the great Author of all things for the preservation of the species. This the Negroes, without doubt, possess in common with the rest of the animal creation, and they indulge it, as inclination prompts, in an almost promiscuous intercourse with the other sex; or at least in temporary connections, which they form without ceremony, and dissolve without reluctance. When age indeed begins to mitigate the ardour, and lessen the fickleness of youth, many of them form attachments, which, strengthened by habit, and endeared by the consciousness of mutual imbecility, produce a union for life. It is not uncommon to behold a venerable couple of this stamp, who, tottering under the load of years, contribute to each other's comfort, with a chearful assiduity which is at once amiable and affecting.

The situation of the aged among the Negroes is indeed commonly such as to make them some amends for the hardships and sufferings of their youth. The labour required of the men is seldom any thing more than to guard the provision-grounds; and the women are chiefly employed in attending the children, in nursing the sick, or in other easy avocations; but their happiness chiefly arises from the high veneration in which old age is held by the Negroes in general, and this I consider as one of the few pleasing traits in their character. In addressing such of their fellow-servants as are any ways advanced in years, they prefix to their names the appellation of Parent, as *Ta* Quaco, and *Ma* Quasheba; *Ta* and *Ma*, signifying Father and Mother, by which designation they mean to convey not only the idea of filial reverence, but also that of esteem and fondness. Neither is the regard thus displayed towards the aged, confined to outward ceremonies and terms of respect alone. It is founded on an active principle of native benevolence, furnishing one of the few exceptions to their general unrelenting and selfish character. The whole body of Negroes on a plantation must be reduced to a deplorable state of wretchedness, if, at any time, they suffer their aged companions to want the common necessaries of life, or even many of its comforts, as far as they can procure them. They seem to me to be actuated on these occasions by a kind of involuntary impulse, operating as a primitive law of nature, which scorns to wait the cold dictates of reason: among them, it is the exercise of a common duty, which courts no observation, and looks for no applause.

Among other propensities and qualities of the Negroes must not be omitted their loquaciousness. They are as fond of exhibiting set speeches, as orators by profession; but it requires a considerable share of patience to hear them throughout; for they commonly make a long preface before they come to the point; beginning with a tedious enumeration of their past services and hardships. They dwell with peculiar energy (if the fact admits it) on the number of children they have presented to *Massa* (*Master*) after which they recapitulate some of the instances of particular kindness shewn them by their owner or employer, adducing these also as proofs of their own merit;

it being evident, they think, that no such kindness can be gratuitous. This is their usual exordium, as well when they bring complaints against others, as when they are called upon to defend themselves; and it is in vain to interrupt either plaintiff or defendant. Yet I have sometimes heard them convey much strong meaning in a narrow compass: I have been surprised by such figurative expressions, and (notwithstanding their ignorance of abstract terms) such pointed sentences, as would have reflected no disgrace on poets and philosophers. One instance recurs to my memory, of so significant a turn of expression in a common labouring Negro, who could have had no opportunity of improvement from the conversation of White people, as is alone, I think, sufficient to demonstrate that Negroes have minds very capable of observation. It was a servant who had brought me a letter, and, while I was preparing an answer, had, through weariness and fatigue, fallen asleep on the floor: as soon as the papers were ready, I directed him to be awakened; but this was no easy matter. When the Negro who attempted to awake him, exclaimed in the usual jargon, *You no hear Massa call you?* that is, Don't you hear Master call you? *Sleep*, replied the poor fellow, looking up, and returning composedly to his slumbers, *Sleep hab no Massa.* (Sleep has no Master.)

Of those imitative arts in which perfection can be attained only in an improved state of society, it is natural to suppose that the Negroes have but little knowledge. An opinion prevails in Europe that they possess organs peculiarly adapted to the science of musick; but this I believe is an ill-founded idea. In vocal harmony they display neither variety nor compass. Nature seems in this respect to have dealt more penuriously by them than towards the rest of the human race. As practical musicians, some of them, by great labour and careful instruction, become sufficiently expert to bear an under-part in a publick concert; but I do not recollect ever to have seen or heard of a Negro who could truly be called a fine performer on any capital instrument. In general they prefer a loud and long-continued noise to the finest harmony, and frequently consume the whole night *in beating on a board with a stick.* This is in fact one of their chief musical instruments; besides which, they have the *Banja* or *Merriwang*, the *Dundo*, and the *Goombay*; all of African origin. The first is an imperfect kind of violincello; except that it is played on by the finger like the guitar; producing a dismal monotony of four notes. The Dundo is precisely a tabor; and the Goombay is a rustick drum; being formed of the trunk of a hollow tree, one end of which is covered with a sheep's skin. From such instruments nothing like a regular tune can be expected, nor is it attempted.

Their songs are commonly *impromptu*, and there are among them individuals who resemble the *improvisutore*, or extempore bards, of Italy; but I cannot say much for their poetry. Their tunes in general are characteristick of their national manners; those of the Eboes being soft and languishing; of the Koromantyns heroick and martial. At the same time, there is observable, in most of them, a predominant melancholy, which, to a man of feeling, is sometimes very affecting.

At their merry meetings, and midnight festivals, they are not without ballads of another kind, adapted to such occasions; and here they give full scope to a talent for ridicule and derision, which is exercised not only against each other, but also, not unfrequently, at the expence of their owner or employer; but most part of their songs at these places are fraught with obscene ribaldry, and accompanied with dances in the highest degree licentious and wanton.

At other times, more especially at the burial of such among them as were respected in life, or venerable through age, they exhibit a sort of *Pyrrhick* or warlike dance, in which their bodies are strongly agitated by running, leaping and jumping, with many violent and frantick gestures and contortions. Their funeral songs too are all of the heroick or martial cast; affording some colour to the prevalent notion, that the Negroes consider death not only as a welcome and happy release from the calamities of their condition, but also as a passport to the place of their nativity; a deliverance which, while it frees them from bondage, restores them to the society of their dearest, long-lost, and lamented relatives in Africa. But I am afraid that this, like other European notions concerning the Negroes, is the dream of poetry; the sympathetick effusion of a fanciful or too credulous an imagination. The Negroes, in general, are so far from courting death, that, among such of them as have resided any length of time in the West Indies, suicide is much less frequent than among the free-born, happy, and civilised inhabitants of Great Britain.

Thomas Carlyle, The Nigger Question, 1849

West-Indian affairs, as we all know, and as some of us know to our cost, are in a rather troublous condition this good while. In regard to West-Indian affairs, however, Lord John Russell is able to comfort us with one fact, indisputable where so many are dubious, That the Negroes are all very happy and doing well. A fact very comfortable indeed. West-Indian Whites, it is admitted, are far enough from happy; West-Indian Colonies not unlike sinking wholly into ruin: at home too, the British Whites are rather badly off; several millions of them hanging on the verge of continual famine; and in single towns, many thousands of them very sore put to it, at this time, not to live "well" or as a man should, in any sense temporal or spiritual, but to live at all:—these, again, are uncomfortable facts; and they are extremely extensive and important ones. But, thank Heaven, our interesting Black population,—equalling almost in number of heads one of the Ridings of Yorkshire, and in *worth* (in quantity of intellect, faculty, docility, energy, and available human valour and value) perhaps one of the streets of Seven Dials,—are all doing remarkably well. "Sweet blighted lilies," —as the American epitaph on the Nigger child has it,—sweet blighted lilies, they are holding-up their heads again! How pleasant, in the universal bankruptcy abroad, and dim dreary stagnancy at home, as if for England too there remained nothing but to suppress Chartist riots, banish united Irishmen, vote the supplies, and *wait* with arms crossed till black Anarchy and Social Death devoured us also, as it has done the others; how pleasant to have always this fact to fall-back upon: Our beautiful Black darlings are at last happy; with little labour except to the teeth, *which* surely, in those excellent horse-jaws of theirs, will not fail!

Our West-Indian Legislatings, with their spoutings, anti-spoutings, and interminable jangle and babble; our Twenty millions down on the nail for Blacks of our own; Thirty gradual millions more, and many brave British lives to boot, in watching Blacks of other people's; and now at last our ruined sugar-estates, differential sugar-duties, "immigration loan," and beautiful Blacks sitting there up to the ears in pumpkins, and doleful Whites sitting here without potatoes to eat: never till now, I think, did the sun look-down on such a jumble of human nonsenses;—of which, with the two hot nights of the Missing-Despatch Debate, God grant that the measure might now at last be full! But no, it is not yet full; we have a long way to travel back, and terrible flounderings to make, and in fact an immense load of nonsense to dislodge from our poor heads, and manifold cobwebs to rend from our poor eyes, before we get into the road again, and can begin to act as serious men that have work to do in this Universe, and no longer as windy sentimentalists that merely have speeches to deliver and despatches to write. O Heaven, in West-Indian matters, and in all manner of matters, it is so with us: the more is the sorrow!—

The West Indies, it appears, are short of labour; as indeed is very conceivable in those circumstances. Where a Black man, by working about half-an-hour a-day (such is the calculation), can supply himself, by aid of sun and soil, with as much pumpkin as will suffice, he is likely to be a little stiff to raise into hard work! Supply and demand, which, science says, should be brought to bear on him, have an uphill task of it with such a man. Strong sun supplies itself gratis, rich soil in those unpeopled or half-peopled regions almost gratis; these are *his* "supply;" and half-an-hour a-day, directed upon these, will produce pumpkin, which is his "demand." The fortunate Black man, very swiftly does he settle *his* account with supply and demand:—not so swiftly the less fortunate White man of those tropical localities. A bad case, his, just now. He himself cannot work; and his black neighbour, rich in pumpkin, is in no haste to help him. Sunk to the ears in pumpkin, imbibing saccharine juices, and much at his ease in the Creation, he can listen to the less fortunate white man's "demand," and take his own time in supplying it. Higher wages, massa; higher, for your cane-crop cannot wait; still higher,—till no conceivable opulence of cane-crop will cover such wages. In Demerara, as I read in the Blue-book of last year, the cane-crop, far and wide, stands rotting; the fortunate black gentlemen, strong in their pumpkins, having all struck till the "demand" rise a little. Sweet blighted lilies, now getting-up their heads again!

Science, however, has a remedy still. Since the demand is so pressing, and the supply so inadequate (equal in fact to *nothing* in some places, as appears), increase the supply; bring more Blacks into the labour-market, then will the rate fall, says science. Not the least surprising part of our West-India-policy is this recipe of "immigration;" of keeping-down the labour-market in those islands by importing new Africans to labour and live there. If the Africans that are already there could be made to lay-down their pumpkins, and labour for their living, there are already Africans enough. If the new Africans, after labouring a little, take to pumpkins like the others, what remedy is there? To bring-in new and ever new Africans, say you, till pumpkins themselves grow dear; till the country is crowded with Africans; and black men there, like white men here, are forced by hunger to labour for their living? That will be a consummation. To have "emancipated" the West Indies into a *Black Ireland*; "free" indeed, but an Ireland, and Black! The world may yet see prodigies; and reality be stranger than a nightmare dream.

And first, with regard to the West Indies, it may be laid-down as a principle, which no eloquence in Exeter Hall, or Westminster Hall, or elsewhere, can invalidate or hide, except for a short time only, That no Black man who will not work according to what ability the gods have given him for working, has the smallest right to eat pumpkin, or to any fraction of land that will grow pumpkin, however plentiful such land may be; but has an indisputable and perpetual *right* to be compelled, by the real proprietors of said land, to do competent work for his living. This is the everlasting duty of all men, black or white, who are born into this world. To do competent work, to labour honestly according to the ability given them; for that and for no other purpose was each one of us sent into this world; and woe is to every man who, by friend or by foe, is prevented from fulfilling this the end of his being. That is the "unhappy" lot: lot equally unhappy cannot otherwise be provided for man. Whatsoever prohibits or prevents a man from this his sacred appointment to labour while he lives on earth,—that, I say, is the man's deadliest enemy; and all men are called upon to do what is in their power or opportunity towards delivering him from that. If it be his own indolence that prevents and prohibits him, then his own indolence is the enemy he must be delivered from: and the first "right" he has,—poor indolent blockhead, black or white,—is, That every *un*prohibited man, whatsoever wiser, more industrious person may be passing that way, shall endeavour to "emancipate" him from his indolence, and by some wise means, as I said, compel him, since inducing will not serve, to do the work he is fit for. Induce him, if you can: yes, sure enough, by all means try what inducement will do; and indeed every coachman and carman knows that secret, without our preaching, and applies it to his very horses as the true method:—but if your Nigger will not be induced? In that case, it is full certain, he must be compelled; should and must; and the tacit prayer he makes (unconsciously he, poor blockhead), to you, and to me, and to all the world who are wiser than himself, is, "Compel me!" For indeed he *must*, or else do and suffer worse,—he as well as we. It were better the work did come out of him! It was the meaning of the gods with him and with us, that his gift should turn to use in this Creation, and not lie poisoning the thoroughfares, as a rotten mass of idleness, agreeable to neither heaven nor earth. For idleness does, in all cases, inevitably *rot*, and become putrescent;—and I say deliberately, the very Devil is in *it*.

None of you, my friends, have been in Demerara lately, I apprehend? May none of you go till matters mend there a little! Under the sky there are uglier sights than perhaps were seen hitherto! Dead corpses, the rotting body of a brother man, whom fate or unjust men have killed, this is not a pleasant spectacle; but what say you to the dead soul of a man,—in a body which still pretends to be vigorously alive, and can drink rum? An idle White gentleman is not pleasant to me; though I confess the real work for him is not easy to find, in these our epochs; and perhaps he is seeking, poor soul, and may find at last. But what say you to an idle Black gentleman, with his rum-bottle in his hand (for a little additional pumpkin you can have red-herrings and rum, in Demerara),—rum-bottle in his hand, no breeches on his body, pumpkin at discretion, and the fruitfulest region of the earth going back to jungle round him? Such things the sun looks-down upon in our fine times; and I, for one, would rather have no hand in them.

Do I, then, hate the Negro? No; except when the soul is killed out of him, I decidedly like poor Quashee; and find him a pretty kind of man. With a pennyworth of oil, you can make a handsome glossy thing of Quashee, when the soul is not killed in him! A swift, supple fellow; a merry-hearted, grinning, dancing, singing, affectionate kind of creature, with a great deal of melody and amenability in his composition. This certainly is a notable fact: The black African, alone of wild-men, can live among men civilised. While all manner of Caribs and others pine into annihilation in presence of the pale faces, he contrives to continue; does not die of sullen irreconcilable rage, of rum, of brutish laziness and darkness, and fated incompatibility with his new place; but lives and multiplies, and evidently means to abide among us, if we can find the right regulation for him. We shall have to find it; we are now engaged in the search; and have at least discovered that of two methods, the old Demerara method, and the new Demerara method, neither will answer.

If precisely the Wisest Man were at the top of society, and the next-wisest next, and so on till we reached the Demerara Nigger (from whom downwards, through the horse, &c., there is no question hitherto), then were this a perfect world, the extreme *maximum* of wisdom produced in it. That is how you might produce your maximum, would some god assist. And I can tell you also how the *minimum* were producible. Let no man in particular be put at the top; let all men be accounted equally wise and worthy, and the notion get abroad that anybody or nobody will do well enough at the top; that money (to which may be added success in stump-oratory) is the real symbol of wisdom, and supply-and-demand the all-sufficient substitute for command and obedience among two-legged animals of the unfeathered class: accomplish all those remarkable convictions in your thinking department; and then in your practical, as is fit, decide by count of heads, the vote of a Demerara Nigger equal and no more to that of a Chancellor Bacon: this, I perceive, will (so soon as it is fairly under way, and *all* obstructions left behind) give the *minimum* of wisdom in your proceedings. Thus were your minimum producible,— with no God needed to assist, nor any Demon even, except the general Demon of *Ignavia* (Unvalour), lazy Indifference to the production or non-production of such things, which runs in our own blood. Were it beautiful, think you? Folly in such million-fold majority, at length peaceably supreme in this earth. Advancing on you as the huge buffalo-phalanx does in the Western Deserts; or as, on a smaller scale, those bristly creatures did in the Country of the Gadarenes. Rushing, namely, in wild *stampede* (the Devil being in them, some small fly having stung them), boundless,—one wing on that edge of your horizon, the other wing on that, and rearward whole tides and oceans of them:—so could Folly rush; the enlightened public one huge Gadarenes-swinery, tail cocked, snout in air, with joyful animating short squeak; fast and ever faster; down steep places, —to the sea of Tiberias, and the bottomless cloacas of Nature: quenched there, since nowhere sooner. My friends, such sight is *too* sublime, if you are out in it, and are not of it!—

I say, if the Black gentleman is born to be a servant, and, in fact, is useful in God's creation only as a servant, then let him hire not by the month, but by a very much longer term. That he be "hired for life,"—really here is the essence of the position he now holds! Consider that matter. All else is abuse in it, and this only is essence;—and the abuses must be cleared away. They must and shall! Yes; and the thing itself seems to offer (its abuses once cleared away) a possibility of the most precious kind for the Black man and for us. Servants hired for life, or by a contract for a long period, and not easily dissoluble; so and not otherwise would all reasonable mortals, Black and White, wish to hire and to be hired! I invite you to reflect on that; for you will find it true. And if true, it is important for us, in reference to this Negro Question and some others.

For the rest, I never thought the "rights of Negroes" worth much discussing, nor the rights of men in any form; the grand point, as I once said, is the *mights* of men,—what portion of their "rights" they have a chance of getting sorted out, and realised, in this confused world. We will not go deep into the question here about the Negro's rights. We will give a single glance into it, and see, for one thing, how complex it is.

West-India Islands, still full of waste fertility, produce abundant pumpkins: pumpkins, however, you will observe, are not the sole requisite for human well-being. No; for a pig they are the one thing needful; but for a man they are only the first of several things needful.

And now observe, my friends, it was not Black Quashee, or those he represents, that made those West-India Islands what they are, or can, by any hypothesis, be considered to have the right of growing pumpkins there. For countless ages, since they first mounted oozy, on the back of earthquakes, from their dark bed in the Ocean deeps, and reeking saluted the tropical Sun, and ever onwards till the European white man first saw them some three short centuries ago, those Islands had produced mere jungle, savagery, poison-reptiles and swamp-malaria: till the white European first saw them, they were as if not yet created,—their noble elements of cinnamon, sugar, coffee, pepper black and gray, lying all asleep, waiting the white enchanter who should say to them, Awake! Till the end of human history and the sounding of the Trump of Doom, they might have lain so, had Quashee and the like of him been the only artists in the game. Swamps, fever-jungles, man-eating Caribs, rattle-snakes, and reeking waste and putrefaction, this had been the produce of them under the incompetent Caribal (what we call Cannibal) possessors, till that time; and Quashee knows, himself, whether ever he could have introduced an improvement. Him, had he by a miraculous chance been wafted thither, the Caribals would have eaten, rolling him as a fat morsel under their tongue; for him, till the sounding of the Trump of Doom, the rattlesnakes and savageries would have held-on their way. It was not he, then; it was another than he! Never by art of his could one pumpkin have grown there to solace any human throat; nothing but savagery and reeking putrefaction could have grown there. These plentiful pumpkins, I say therefore, are not his: no, they are another's; they are his only under conditions. Conditions which Exeter Hall, for the present, has forgotten; but which Nature and the Eternal Powers have by no manner of means forgotten, but do at all moments keep in mind; and, at the right moment, will, with the due impressiveness, perhaps in a rather terrible manner, bring again to our mind also!

If Quashee will not honestly aid in bringing-out those sugars, cinnamons and nobler products of the West-Indian Islands, for the benefit of all mankind, then I say neither will the Powers permit Quashee to continue growing pumpkins there for his own lazy benefit; but will shear him out, by and by, like a lazy gourd overshadowing rich ground; him and all that partake with him,—perhaps in a very terrible manner.

Fair towards Britain it will be, that Quashee give work for privilege to grow pumpkins. Not a pumpkin, Quashee, not a square yard of soil, till you agree to do the State so many days of service. Annually that soil will grow you pumpkins; but annually also, without fail, shall you, for the owner thereof, do your appointed days of labour. The State has plenty of waste soil; but the State will religiously give you none of it on other terms. The State wants sugar from these Islands, and means to have it; wants virtuous industry in these Islands, and must have it. The State demands of you such service as will bring these results, this latter result which includes all. Not a Black Ireland, by immigration, and boundless black supply for the demand; not that,—may the gods forbid!—but a regulated

West Indies, with black working population in adequate numbers; all "happy," if they find it possible; and *not* entirely unbeautiful to gods and men, which latter result they *must* find possible! All "happy" enough; that is to say, all working according to the faculty they have got, making a little more divine this Earth which the gods have given them. Is there any other "happiness,"—if it be not that of pigs fattening daily to the slaughter? So will the State speak by and by.

Any poor idle Black man, any idle White man, rich or poor, is a mere eye-sorrow to the State; a perpetual blister on the skin of the State. The State is taking measures, some of them rather extensive, in Europe at this very time, and already, as in Paris, Berlin and elsewhere, rather tremendous measures, to *get* its rich white men set to work; for alas, they also have long sat Negro-like up to the ears in pumpkin, regardless of 'work,' and of a world all going to waste for their idleness!

Anthony Trollope, The West Indies and the Spanish Main, 1859

To an Englishman who has never lived in a slave country, or in a country in which slavery once prevailed, the negro population is of course the most striking feature of the West Indies. But the eye soon becomes accustomed to the black skin and the thick lip, and the ear to the broken patois which is the nearest approach to English which the ordinary negro ever makes. When one has been a week among them, the novelty is all gone. It is only by an exercise of memory and intellect that one is enabled to think of them as a strange race.

But how strange is the race of Creole negroes—of negroes, that is, born out of Africa! They have no country of their own, yet have they not hitherto any country of their adoption; for, whether as slaves in Cuba, or as free labourers in the British isles, they are in each case a servile people in a foreign land. They have no language of their own, nor have they as yet any language of their adoption; for they speak their broken English as uneducated foreigners always speak a foreign language.

They have no idea of country, and no pride of race; for even among themselves, the word "nigger" conveys their worst term of reproach. They have no religion of their own, and can hardly as yet be said to have, as a people, a religion by adoption; and yet there is no race which has more strongly developed its own physical aptitudes and inaptitudes, its own habits, its own tastes, and its own faults.

The West Indian negro knows nothing of Africa except that it is a term of reproach. If African immigrants are put to work on the same estate with him, he will not eat with them, or drink with them, or walk with them. He will hardly work beside them, and regards himself as a creature immeasurably the superior of the new comer. But yet he has made no approach to the civilization of his white fellow-creature, whom he imitates as a monkey does a man.

Physically he is capable of the hardest bodily work, and that probably with less bodily pain than men of any other race; but he is idle, unambitious as to worldly position, sensual, and content with little. Intellectually, he is apparently capable of but little sustained effort; but, singularly enough, here he is ambitious. He burns to be regarded as a scholar, puzzles himself with fine words, addicts himself to religion for the sake of appearance, and delights in aping the little graces of civilization. He despises himself thoroughly, and would probably be content to starve for a month if he could appear as a white man for a day; but yet he delights in signs of respect paid to him, black man as he is, and is always thinking of his own dignity. If you want to win his heart for an hour, call him a gentleman; but if you want to reduce him to a despairing obedience, tell him that he is a filthy nigger, assure him that his father and mother had tails like monkeys, and forbid him to think that he can have a soul like a white man. Among the West Indies one may frequently see either course adopted towards them by their unreasoning ascendant masters.

I do not think that education has as yet done much for the black man in the Western world. He can always observe, and often read; but he can seldom reason. I do not mean to assert that he is absolutely without mental power, as a calf is. He does draw conclusions, but he carries them only a short way. I think that he seldom understands the purpose of industry, the object of truth, or the results of honesty. He is not always idle, perhaps not always false, certainly not always a thief; but his motives are the fear of immediate punishment, or hopes of immediate reward. He fears that and hopes that only. Certain virtues he copies, because they are the virtues of a white man. The white man is the god present to his eye, and he believes in him—believes in him with a qualified faith, and imitates him with a qualified constancy.

And thus I am led to say, and I say it with sorrow enough, that I distrust the negro's religion. What I mean is this: that in my opinion they rarely take in and digest the great and simple doctrines of Christianity, that they should love and fear the Lord their God, and love their neighbours as themselves.

Those who differ from me—and the number will comprise the whole clergy of these western realms, and very many beside the clergy—will ask, among other questions, whether these simple doctrines are obeyed in England much better than they are in Jamaica. I would reply that I am not speaking of obedience. The opinion which I venture to give is, that the very first meaning of the terms does not often reach the negro's mind, not even the minds of those among them who are enthusiastically religious. To them religious exercises are in themselves the good thing desirable. They sing their psalms, and believe, probably, that good will result; but they do not connect their psalms with the practice of any virtue. They say their prayers; but, having said them, have no idea that they should therefore forgive offences. They hear the commandments and delight in the responses; but those commandments are not in their hearts connected with abstinence from adultery or calumny. They delight to go to church or meeting; they are energetic in singing psalms; they are constant in the responses; and, which is saying much more for them, they are wonderfully expert at Scripture texts; but—and I say it with grief of heart, and with much trembling also at the reproaches which I shall have to endure—I doubt whether religion does often reach their minds.

In many respects the negro's phase of humanity differs much from that which is common to us, and which has been produced by our admixture of blood and our present extent of civilization. They are more passionate than the white men, but rarely vindictive, as we are. The smallest injury excites their eager wrath, but no injury produces sustained hatred. In the same way, they are seldom grateful, though often very thankful. They are covetous of notice as is a child or a dog; but they have little idea of earning continual respect. They best love him who is most unlike themselves, and they despise the coloured man who approaches them in breed. When they have once recognized a man as their master, they will be faithful to him; but the more they fear that master, the more they will respect him. They have no care for to-morrow, but they delight in being gaudy for to-day. Their crimes are those of momentary impulse, as are also their virtues. They fear death; but if they can lie in the sun without pain for the hour they will hardly drag themselves to the hospital, though their disease be mortal. They love their offspring, but in their rage will ill use them fearfully. They are proud of them when they are praised, but will sell their daughter's virtue for a dollar. They are greedy of food, but generally indifferent as to its quality. They rejoice in finery, and have in many cases begun to understand the benefit of comparative cleanliness; but they are rarely tidy. A little makes them happy, and nothing makes them permanently wretched. On the whole, they laugh and sing and sleep through life; and if life were all, they would not have so bad a time of it.

These, I think, are the qualities of the negro. Many of them are in their way good; but are they not such as we have generally seen in the lower spheres of life?

Much of this is strongly opposed to the idea of the Creole negro which has lately become prevalent in England. He has been praised for his piety, and especially praised for his consistent gratitude to his benefactors and faithful adherence to his master's interests.

On such subjects our greatest difficulty is perhaps that of avoiding an opinion formed by exceptional cases. That there are and have been pious negroes I do not doubt. That many are strongly tinctured with the language and outward bearing of piety I am well aware. I know that they love the Bible— love it as the Roman Catholic girl loves the doll of a Madonna which she dresses with muslin and ribbons. In a certain sense this is piety, and such piety they often possess.

And I do not deny their family attachments; but it is the attachment of a dog. We have all had dogs whom we have well used, and have prided ourselves on their fidelity. We have seen them to be wretched when they lose us for a moment, and have smiled at their joy when they again discover us. We have noted their patience as they wait for food from the hand they know will feed them. We have seen with delight how their love for us glistens in their eyes. We trust them with our children as the safest playmates, and teach them in mocking sport the tricks of humanity. In return for this, the dear brutes give us all their hearts, but it is not given in gratitude; and they abstain with all their power from injury and offence, but they do not abstain from judgment. Let his master ill use his dog ever so cruelly, yet the animal has no anger against him when the pain is over. Let a stranger save him from such ill usage, and he has no thankfulness after the moment. Affection and fidelity are things of custom with him.

I know how deep will be the indignation I shall draw upon my head by this picture of a fellow-creature and a fellow-Christian. Man's philanthropy would wish to look on all men as walking in a quick path towards the perfection of civilization. And men are not happy in their good efforts unless they themselves can see their effects. They are not content to fight for the wellbeing of a race, and to think that the victory shall not come till the victors shall for centuries have been mingled with the dust. The friend of the negro, when he puts his shoulder to the wheel, and tries to rescue his black brother from the degradation of an inferior species, hopes to see his client rise up at once with all the glories of civilization round his head.

But to return to our sable friends. The first desire of a man in a state of civilization is for property. Greed and covetousness are no doubt vices; but they are the vices which have grown from cognate virtues. Without a desire for property, man could make no progress. But the negro has no such desire; no desire strong enough to induce him to labour for that which he wants. In order that he may eat to-day and be clothed tomorrow, he will work a little; as for anything beyond that, he is content to lie in the sun.

Emancipation and the last change in the sugar duties have made land only too plentiful in Jamaica, and enormous tracts have been thrown out of cultivation as unprofitable. And it is also only too fertile. The negro, consequently, has had unbounded facility of squatting, and has availed himself of it freely. To recede from civilization and become again savage— as savage as the laws of the community will permit—has been to his taste. I believe that he would altogether retrograde if left to himself.

I shall now be asked, having said so much, whether I think that emancipation was wrong. By no means. I think that emancipation was clearly right; but I think that we expected far too great and far too quick a result from emancipation.

These people are a servile race, fitted by nature for the hardest physical work, and apparently at present fitted for little else. Some thirty years since they were in a state when such work was their lot; but their tasks were exacted from them in a condition of bondage abhorrent to the feelings of the age, and opposed to the religion which we practised. For us, thinking as we did, slavery was a sin. From that sin we have cleansed ourselves. But the mere fact of doing so has not freed us from our difficulties. Nor was it to be expected that it should. The discontinuance of a sin is always the commencement of a struggle.

And who can blame the black man? He is free to work, or free to let it alone. He can live without work and roll in the sun, and suck oranges and eat bread-fruit; ay, and ride a horse perhaps, and wear a white waistcoat and plaited shirt on Sundays. Why should he care for the busher? I will not dig cane-holes for half a crown a day; and why should I expect him to do so? I can live without it; so can he.

But, nevertheless, it would be very well if we could so contrive that he should not live without work. It is clearly not Nature's intention that he should be exempted from the general lot of Adam's children. We would not have our friend a slave; but we would fain force him to give the world a fair day's work for his fair day's provender if we knew how to do so without making him a slave. The fact I take it is, that there are too many good things in Jamaica for the number who have to enjoy them. If the competitors were more in number, more trouble would be necessary in their acquirement.

And now, just at this moment, philanthropy is again busy in England protecting the Jamaica negro. He is a man and a brother, and shall we not regard him? Certainly, my philanthropic friend, let us regard him well. He *is* a man; and, if you will, a brother; but he is the very idlest brother with which a hardworking workman was ever cursed, intent only on getting his mess of pottage without giving anything in return. His petitions about the labour market, my excellently-softhearted friend, and his desire to be protected from undue competition are—. Oh, my friend, I cannot tell you how utterly they are—gammon. He is now eating his yam without work, and in that privilege he is anxious to be maintained. And you, are you willing to assist him in his views?

The negro slave was ill treated—ill treated, at any rate, in that he was a slave; and therefore, by that reaction which prevails in all human matters, it is now thought necessary to wrap him up in cotton and put him under a glass case. The wind must not blow on him too roughly, and the rose-leaves on which he sleeps should not be ruffled. He has been a slave; therefore now let him be a Sybarite. His father did an ample share of work; therefore let the son be made free from his portion in the primeval curse. The friends of the negro, if they do not actually use such arguments, endeavour to carry out such a theory.

CHAPTER 7

The Humanitarian Impulse

English sentiment against black slavery began with a group of talented philanthropists who undertook, from the mid-eighteenth century, to enlighten public opinion about the Negro and, with educated opinion behind them, to pressurise Parliament into restoring freedom to the slaves throughout the empire.

Granville Sharp (1735–1813) gave to the humanitarian impulse in England a shape and direction previously lacking. The extract below, from one of Sharp's many tracts, resulted directly from his involvement with slaves in London. In 1765 Sharp had rescued a maltreated slave, Jonathan Strong, who two years later was recaptured and put in jail. Sharp again rescued him. Jonathan Strong's 'owner', David Lisle, then took legal action against Sharp who was advised by his lawyers that, in view of the Yorke-Talbot opinion of 1729, the law was probably on the side of Lisle. With splendid intransigeance Sharp thereupon plunged into research to prove that slavery in England was in fact unlawful, the result being *A Representation of the Injustice* . . . , published in 1769.[1] Meanwhile Sharp waited patiently for a case that could be brought before a court of law with a reasonable chance of obtaining an authoritative decision against English slavery. His patience was rewarded ultimately with the Somerset case of 1772, in the preliminaries of which he played a crucial role. The major importance of the extract reproduced below lies in the way Sharp directed popular attention to the illegality of slavery in England, a move which was, in its turn, a stepping stone in political organisation and propaganda for abolition and emancipation.

John Wesley (1703–1791) is not generally famous for his anti-slavery sentiments, a fact which speaks for his diversity of talents and achievements, but his role in rallying support for the philanthropist cause was crucial. Wesley's attack on the British involvement in slave-trading, published in 1774,[2] had a huge circulation in the 1780s and was influential in turning the expanding and vociferous body of Methodists against the slave trade. It also led to extensive missionary work in the West Indies. Extracts quoted here contain examples of the telling and precise criticisms that he levelled against the slave trade and reveal quite clearly the sort of audience to which he was appealing. His description of the Negro is perceptive and sympathetic. This restoration of a human image to the Negro played no small part in slowly weighting the scales in favour of the abolitionist cause.

James Ramsay (1773–1789), a naval surgeon, decided to campaign against the evil of slavery after visiting a disease-ridden slaver and being appalled at the treatment of the slaves. Taking Holy Orders, he became a missionary in the West Indies where his success with the slaves was not to the planters' liking. Returning to England, Ramsay produced his *Essay on the Treatment and Conversion of African Slaves . . . '*[3] and joined forces with Wilberforce, Clarkson and the abolitionist Quakers. Selections from this essay, reproduced below, reveal the force of Ramsay's egalitarian treatment of the slave.

Perhaps the greatest of all the abolitionists was Thomas Clarkson (1760–1846) who undertook the back-breaking and frequently dangerous task of gathering evidence against the slave trade from the slave-traders themselves. The extract presented here comes from his prize-winning essay first published in 1785, which he wrote as a student at Cambridge, an *Essay on the Slavery and Commerce of the Human Species.*[4] Its publication provoked a wave of public indignation against the slave traders. Despite other publications in a lifetime's work devoted to the cause of black freedom, the impact of this essay and the sympathy it evoked for the slave was never to be surpassed.

William Dickson's essay, *Letters on Slavery*, published in 1789,[5] took up the theme of the Negro's innate abilities in order to challenge the widespread belief in black inferiority. Dickson had been the secretary to the Governor of Barbados and had seen at first hand the crippling life of slavery. In the extract below he claims that it would be totally impossible for a slave in such conditions to reach the attainments of free men. Planters, he said, failed to see that the qualities they complained of in the slave stemmed directly from the life to which the slaves were subjected.

The activities of William Wilberforce (1759–1833) in the cause of emancipation spanned half a century. The extract below, from his later writings,[6] is chosen to show how the humanitarians were obliged to repeat arguments and evidence that, on rational grounds, should have clinched their case when first presented years before. Like Granville Sharp, Wilberforce campaigned for black freedom at every conceivable level, from the late 1780s to his death on the eve of emancipation.

Granville Sharp, A Representation of the Injustice . . . , 1769

An examination of the Advantages and Disadvantages of tolerating SLAVERY *in England.*

In the two former parts of this work, I have attempted to demonstrate, that Slavery is an innovation in England, contrary to the spirit and intention of our present laws and constitution. If this opinion be admitted, the following points do, of course, demand the serious consideration of the public.

1st. How far this *innovation* may be esteemed necessary? or whether there are any singular advantages attending it, which should engage us to favour the establishment of it here, in direct opposition both to *law and equity?* And 2dly, Whether the same is not liable, on the other hand, to be attended with some such unavoidable mischiefs, as would much over-balance any advantages that can possibly be proposed or expected from it?

F

The only reasonable plea that is usually alledged, for the necessity of Slavery in England, is the security of private property; for it would be unjust (say the advocates for Slavery) that the master's property or right in Slaves, should be determined or varied, by their coming from the West Indies to England.

But before this plea be admitted, we ought to consider the master's reason for bringing a Slave to England.

It cannot be for the sake of a market, to make his money of him, because a stout young Negro, who can read and write, and is approved of in domestic service, is sold for no more than thirty pounds in England; whereas it is certain, that such a one might be sold, at least, for the same sum in the West Indies; and sometimes, perhaps, for near double the money, so that a Slave from thence, not only loads his owner with an additional charge for freight, but is brought to a much worse market.

It is plain therefore, that trade cannot be materially affected, by the putting a stop to such clandestine and unnatural traffic.

And further, if the master brings his Slaves to England, for the sake of their domestic services only, and not for sale, he cannot be said to be really injured, when they regain their liberty; because I will make it appear hereafter, that he may be served, during his stay in England, full as well, and with as little expence, by free English servants, as he could possibly be by his own Slaves, even if the law would permit him to keep them as such.

But suppose the master, by the prejudices of a West Indian education, is so capricious and depraved, that he prefers the constrained service of Slaves to the willing attendance of freemen. Or rather, let us suppose another case, viz.

That a West Indian gentleman comes to England on account of his health, and is *obliged* to bring some Slaves with him, to attend him during the voyage, and that it might perhaps be very inconvenient to lose them on his arrival here.

Now in both these cases there is still a remedy left, which may enable the former supposed person to indulge, in some measure, his capricious humour, and the latter to suit his convenience or necessity, without infringing further upon the civil liberties of this kingdom, than what the laws will warrant.

For when any West Indian gentleman intends to remove to England, he may undoubtedly find a sufficient number of his Slaves, that would gladly enter into a *written agreement*, to return to the West Indies from England, when required, merely for the sake of coming to England.

It must be remembered however, that a previous manumission will be necessary, otherwise there can be no legal agreement whatsoever for service; because a Slave who has signed an agreement, may afterwards plead *illegal duress per minas*, &c. which will effectually invalidate his contract in England.

But perhaps it may be objected, that the granting of a manumission is prohibited in the colonies by law.

. . . Nevertheless I apprehend, that when the service of an approved Slave is become so necessary to his master, that it cannot, without great inconvenience, be dispensed with; the same ought to be esteemed a *meritorious service*, such as the Governor and Council cannot reasonably disallow.

So that I do not think, a master would find any great difficulty in procuring leave to set free such persons, as he should think necessary *to carry with him out of the colony*; because no man could object, that the granting of a manumission in this case, is liable to affect the safety of the colony, even in the least degree.

But there is still another very obvious and natural objection to be removed, before my proposal of a contract can possibly be admitted, viz. That no Slave, after being once made free, would *willingly* enter again into bondage by signing a contract,

This objection would certainly hold good in England, or in any other free country; but the tyrannical constitution of the British colonies (to the indelible disgrace of the British name) reduces the freedom of any poor man to so low a value, that a bargain for the servitude of such a one, by indenture, might be made on very easy terms, so far is it from being unnatural, or even uncommon; therefore the same objection cannot be said to subsist in the colonies. . . . And when this precaution of a written agreement is taken, the indentured Slaves will indeed remain the private property of their masters for the term of their contracts, even in England, (as I have before remarked) and the masters *"may legally compel them to return again to the plantations"* by virtue of the xiiith sect. of the Habeas Corpus act, provided that they do not *unlawfully* confine or hurt their persons.

... But suppose a Slave should absolutely refuse to enter into such *a written agreement*, and yet the service of that Slave, either on account of his known fidelity or capacity, is become so necessary to the master, that he cannot easily dispense with it. Whenever this happens to be the case, the master will be apt to think himself much aggrieved by the civil liberty and custom of England, which deprives him of the *constrained service* of his useful Slave, but for my part, I think it cannot be esteemed an unreasonable hardship upon the master, that he should be obliged to make it the interest of such a very useful person, to serve and attend him willingly, though it should be at the expence even of the highest rate of Servants wages (beside the loss of property by the manumission) *"for the Labourer is worthy of his hire"*.

I do not apprehend, that the above supposed case will be very general, but if it should, 'tis certainly better, that some hardship should lie upon those selfish masters, who might be ungenerous enough *to think it a hardship*, than that a real and national inconvenience should be felt, by permitting every person (without any inconvenience to himself) to increase the present stock of black Servants in this kingdom, which is already much too numerous. Therefore, even if there should be really any inconvenience or hardship upon the master, contrary or different to what I have supposed, 'tis certainly not to be lamented, because the public good seems to require some restraint of this unnatural increase of black subjects.

Though the advocates for Slavery should set forth their plea of PRIVATE PROPERTY (the only plea they can alledge with any the least appearance of justice) in the very best light that it is capable of, yet I flatter myself, that the foregoing considerations will be sufficient to balance it: because A PRIVATE PROPERTY, *which is unnatural in itself, inconvenient* and *hurtful to the public*, and (above all) plainly *contrary to the laws and constitu-*

tions of this kingdom, cannot justly be otherwise esteemed, *than as* A PRIVATE PROPERTY *in contraband goods,* the forfeiture of which, no good citizen ought to regret.

It cannot reasonably be alledged, that the service of Slaves is necessary in England, whilst so many of our own free fellow-subjects want bread.

If the English labourer is not able, with hard work, to earn more than what will barely provide him his necessary food and coarse or ragged cloathing, what more can his employer reasonably desire of him, even if he were his Slave?

The mere boarding and cloathing of a Slave in England (if human nature is not depressed and vilified) will undoubtedly be as expensive to the master, as the wages of English labourers, if not more so; because poor men can generally provide for themselves at a cheaper rate, and will put up with inconveniencies (when the same are voluntary), which would really be oppressive, nay, even intolerable, from the hand of another person.

But, besides the necessary charges of eating and cloathing, there are other expences over and above, to which the employer of free labourers is not subject, viz. the prime cost, as well as freight of the Slave; Apothecaries and Surgeons Bills on account of sickness and accidents, and a multitude of other unavoidable articles, which must be defrayed by the master.

Now, though the advocates for Slavery should be obliged to allow this (as I think they must) with respect to labourers, yet perhaps they will still urge, that there is nevertheless a considerable advantage by Slaves, when they are kept as domestics, because no wages are paid, whereas, free Servants are not only cloathed and boarded at the master's expence as well as the others, but receive wages into the bargain.

This reasoning, at first, seems plausible; but on the other hand, let us set off the annual interest of the Slave's price in part of wages, and then divide the principal sum itself into as many portions as the average number of years, that a Slave is usually capable of being useful. Besides this, the uncertainty of health and life, must be thrown into the scale, unless the expense of insurance upon these precarious circumstances be likewise added; otherwise the principal sum itself is laid out on a very bad security.

Now when all these things are weighed and compared with the common rate of Servants wages, there will not appear to be any great saving in the employing of Slaves; especially if it be considered, that healthy and comely boys and girls, the children of our own free fellow-subjects may be procured out of any county in this or the neighbouring kingdoms, to serve as apprentices or servants, for six or seven years or more, without any wages at all; which ought certainly to be remembered, when the average rate of wages to Servants and labourers is mentioned.

Therefore upon the whole, I think it must appear, that the service of Slaves in England, would be quite as expensive, as that of freemen, and consequently, that there cannot be any real advantages in a toleration of Slavery in this kingdom; at least, I am not able to point them out, though I have carefully considered the subject.

A toleration of Slavery is, in effect, a toleration of inhumanity; for there are wretches in the world, who make no scruple to gain, by wearing out their Slaves with continual labour and a scanty allowance, before they have lived out half their natural days. . . .

At present the inhumanity of *constrained labour in excess* extends no farther in England, than to our beasts, as post and hackney horses, sand asses, &c.

But thanks to our laws, and not to the general good disposition of masters, that it is so; for the wretch, who is bad enough to maltreat a helpless beast, would not spare his fellow man, if he had him as much in his power.

The maintenance of civil liberty is therefore absolutely necessary to prevent an increase of our national guilt, by the addition of the horrid crime of tyranny.

It is not my business at present to examine, how far a toleration of Slavery may be necessary or justifiable in the West-Indies. 'Tis sufficient for my purpose, that it is not so here. But notwithstanding, that the plea of necessity cannot here be urged, yet this is no reason, why an increase of the practice is not to be feared. . . .

Also that the prisons of this free city have been frequently prostituted of late by the tyrannical and dangerous practice of confining Negroes, under the pretence of Slavery, though there has been no Warrants whatsoever for their commitment.

This circumstance of confining a man without a warrant, has so great a resemblance to the proceedings of a Popish Inquisition, that it is but too obvious what dangerous practices such scandalous innovations (if permitted to grow more into use) are liable to introduce.

No person can be safe, if wicked and designing men have it in their power, under the pretence of private property as a Slave, to throw a man clandestinely without a warrant into gaol, and to conceal him there, until they can conveniently dispose of him.

A freeman may be thus robbed of his liberty and carried beyond the seas, without having the least opportunity of making his case known; which should teach us how jealous we ought to be of all imprisonments made without the authority or previous examination of the civil magistrate.

The distinction of colour will, in a short time, be no protection against such outrages, especially as not only Negroes, but Mulattos, and even *American Indians*, (which appears by one of the advertisements before quoted) are retained in Slavery in our American colonies; for there are many honest weather-beaten Englishmen, who have as little reason to boast of their complexion as the Indians. And indeed the more northern Indians have no difference from us in complexion, but such as is occasioned by the climate or different way of living. The plea of *private* property, therefore, cannot by any means justify a *private* commitment of any person whatsoever to prison, because of the apparent danger and tendency of such an innovation.

This dangerous practice of concealing in prison, was attempted in the case of Jonathan Strong; for the door keeper of the P—lt—y C—pt—r (or some person who acted for him) absolutely refused for two days to permit this poor injured Negro to be seen or spoke with, though a person went on purpose both those days to demand the same.

However, in excuse for the Londoners, I have the satisfaction to observe, that the practice of Slave-holding is now only in its infancy amongst us; and Slaves are at present employed in no other capacity, than that of Domestic Servants. But if such practices are permitted much longer with impunity, *the evil will take root; precedent and custom will too soon be pleaded in its behalf;* and as Slavery becomes more familiar in our eyes, mercenary and selfish men may take it into their heads, to employ their Slaves (not merely in domestick affairs as at present, but) in husbandry; so that they may think it worth their while to breed them like cattle on their estates, as they do even in the North American colonies, though the children of Slaves, born there, are as much the King's natural born subjects as the free natives of England.

God forbid that this should ever be the case here! However, we cannot be too jealous of every thing that tends to it; lest it should afterwards be remarked, that a *misunderstanding, or mistaken opinion of the lawyers of this age,* has introduced a vassalage much more disgraceful and pernicious, than that which the *ancient lawyers* have so happily abolished.

This is not altogether a chimera. A disposition, howsoever impolitic and unnatural, which prevails in one place, may prevail likewise in another.

The account of the American settlements before quoted, informs us of a certain unnatural disposition of the planters, *"to do every thing by Negroes, which can possibly be done by them,"* notwithstanding that there are wholesome laws to oblige them to keep a certain proportion of white Servants: and the ingenious author observes thereupon, that, *"if this disposition continues, in a little time (which is indeed nearly the case already), all the English in our colonies there will consist of little more than a few planters and merchants; and the rest will be a despicable, though a dangerous, because a numerous and disaffected, herd of African Slaves."*

It would indeed be absurd to conceive, that such a disposition can very soon become general here in England, yet there is no absurdity in supposing a possibility of its being introduced by slow degrees.

All laws ought to be founded upon the principle of *"doing as one would be done by:*" and indeed this principle seems to be the very basis of the English constitution; for what precaution could possibly be more effectual for that purpose, than the right which we enjoy of being *judged by our peers*, creditable persons of the vicinage; especially, as we may likewise claim the right of excepting against any particular jury-man, who might be suspected of partiality?

This law breathes the pure spirit of liberty, equity and social love: being calculated to maintain that consideration and mutual regard, which one person ought to have for another, howsoever unequal in rank or station.

But when any part of the community, under the pretence of *private property*, is deprived of this common privilege, 'tis a violation of civil liberty, which is entirely inconsistent with the social principles of a free state.

True liberty protects the labourer as well as his lord; preserves the dignity of human nature, and seldom fails to render a province rich and populous: whereas on the other hand, a toleration of Slavery is the highest breach of social virtue, and not only tends to depopulation, but too often renders the minds of both masters and Slaves utterly depraved and inhuman, by the hateful extremes of exaltation and depression.

If such a toleration should ever be generally admitted in England, (which God forbid!) we shall no longer deserve to be esteemed a *civilized* people: because, when the customs of *uncivilized* nations, and the *uncivilized customs* which disgrace our own colonies are become so familiar, as to be permitted among us with impunity, we ourselves must insensibly degenerate to the same degree of baseness, with those from whom such bad customs were derived, and may too soon have the mortification to see the *hateful extremes of tyranny and Slavery fostered under every roof.*

Then must the happy medium of *a well regulated liberty* be necessarily compelled to find shelter in some *more civilized* country, where social virtue, and that divine precept, "*thou shalt love thy neighbour as thyself,*" are better understood.

An attempt to prove the dangerous tendency, injustice and

disgrace of tolerating Slavery amongst Englishmen, would in any former age have been esteemed as superfluous and ridiculous, as if a man should undertake in a formal manner, to prove that *darkness* is not *light*.

Sorry am I, that the depravity of the present age has made a demonstration of this kind necessary!

John Wesley, Thoughts Upon Slavery, 1774

IV. 1. This is the plain, unaggravated matter of fact. Such is the manner wherein our African slaves are procured; such the manner wherein they are removed from their native land, and wherein they are treated in our plantations. I would now inquire, whether these things can be defended, on the principles of even heathen honesty; whether they can be reconciled (setting the Bible out of the question) with any degree of either justice or mercy.

2. The grand plea is, "They are authorized by law." But can law, human law, change the nature of things? Can it turn darkness into light, or evil into good? By no means. Notwithstanding ten thousand laws, right is right, and wrong is wrong still. There must still remain an essential difference between justice and injustice, cruelty and mercy. So that I still ask, Who can reconcile this treatment of the Negroes, first and last, with either mercy or justice?

Where is the justice of inflicting the severest evils on those that have done us no wrong? of depriving those that never injured us in word or deed, of every comfort of life? of tearing them from their native country, and depriving them of liberty itself, to which an Angolan has the same natural right as an Englishman, and on which he sets as high a value? Yea, where is the justice of taking away the lives of innocent, inoffensive men; murdering thousands of them in their own land, by the hands of their own countrymen; many thousands, year after year, on shipboard, and then casting them like dung into the sea; and tens of thousands in that cruel slavery to which they are so unjustly reduced?

3. But waving, for the present, all other considerations, I strike at the root of this complicated villany; I absolutely deny all slave-holding to be consistent with any degree of natural justice.

I cannot place this in a clearer light than that great ornament of his profession, Judge Blackstone, has already done. Part of his words are as follows:—

"The three origins of the right of slavery assigned by Justinian, are all built upon false foundations: (1.) Slavery is said to arise from captivity in war. The conqueror having a right to the life of his captives, if he spares that, has then a right to deal with them as he pleases. But this is untrue, if taken generally,—that, by the laws of nations, a man has a right to kill his enemy. He has only a right to kill him in particular cases, in cases of absolute necessity for self-defence. And it is plain, this absolute necessity did not subsist, since he did not kill him, but made him prisoner. War itself is justifiable only on principles of self-preservation: Therefore it gives us no right over prisoners, but to hinder their hurting us by confining them. Much less can it give a right to torture, or kill, or even to enslave an enemy when the war is over. Since therefore the right of making our prisoners slaves, depends on a supposed right of slaughter, that foundation failing, the consequence which is drawn from it must fail likewise.

"It is said, Secondly, slavery may begin by one man's selling himself to another. And it is true, a man may sell himself to work for another; but he cannot sell himself to be a slave, as above defined. Every sale implies an equivalent given to the seller, in lieu of what he transfers to the buyer. But what equivalent can be given for life or liberty? His property likewise, with the very price which he seems to receive, devolves *ipso facto* to his master, the instant he becomes his slave: In this case, therefore, the buyer gives nothing, and the seller receives nothing. Of what validity then can a sale be, which destroys the very principle upon which all sales are founded?

"We are told, Thirdly, that men may be born slaves, by being the children of slaves. But this, being built upon the two former rights, must fall together with them. If neither captivity nor contract can, by the plain law of nature and reason, reduce the parent to a state of slavery, much less can they reduce the offspring." It clearly follows, that all slavery is as irreconcilable to justice as to mercy.

4. That slave-holding is utterly inconsistent with mercy, is almost too plain to need a proof. Indeed, it is said, "that these Negroes being prisoners of war, our captains and factors buy them, merely to save them from being put to death. And is not this mercy?" I answer, (1.) Did Sir John Hawkins, and many others, seize upon men, women, and children, who were at peace in their own fields or houses, merely to save them from death? (2.) Was it to save them from death, that they knocked out the brains of those they could not bring away? (3.) Who occasioned and fomented those wars, wherein these poor creatures were taken prisoners? Who excited them by money, by drink, by every possible means, to fall upon one another? Was it not themselves? They know in their own conscience it was, if they have any conscience left. But, (4.) To bring the matter to a short issue, can they say before God, that they ever took a single voyage, or bought a single Negro, from this motive? They cannot; they well know, to get money, not to save lives, was the whole and sole spring of their motions.

5. But if this manner of procuring and treating Negroes is not consistent either with mercy or justice, yet there is a plea for it which every man of business will acknowledge to be quite sufficient. Fifty years ago, one meeting an eminent Statesman in the lobby of the House of Commons, said, "You have been long talking about justice and equity. Pray which is this bill; equity or justice?" He answered very short and plain, "D—n justice; it is necessity." Here also the slave-holder fixes his foot; here he rests the strength of his cause. "If it is not quite right, yet it must be so; there is an absolute necessity for it. It is necessary we should procure slaves; and when we have procured them, it is necessary to use them with severity, considering their stupidity, stubbornness, and wickedness."

I answer, You stumble at the threshold; I deny that villany

is every necessary. It is impossible that it should ever be necessary for any reasonable creature to violate all the laws of justice, mercy, and truth. No circumstances can make it necessary for a man to burst in sunder all the ties of humanity. It can never be necessary for a rational being to sink himself below a brute. A man can be under no necessity of degrading himself into a wolf. The absurdity of the supposition is so glaring, that one would wonder any one can help seeing it.

6. This in general. But, to be more particular, I ask, First, What is necessary? and, Secondly, To what end? It may be answered, "The whole method now used by the original purchasers of Negroes is necessary to the furnishing our colonies yearly with a hundred thousand slaves." I grant, this is necessary to that end. But how is that end necessary? How will you prove it necessary that one hundred, that one, of those slaves should be procured? "Why, it is necessary to my gaining an hundred thousand pounds." Perhaps so: But how is this necessary? It is very possible you might be both a better and a happier man, if you had not a quarter of it. I deny that your gaining one thousand is necessary either to your present or eternal happiness. "But, however, you must allow, these slaves are necessary for the cultivation of our islands; inasmuch as white men are not able to labour in hot climates." I answer, First, it were better that all those islands should remain uncultivated for ever; yea, it were more desirable that they were altogether sunk in the depth of the sea, than that they should be cultivated at so high a price as the violation of justice, mercy, and truth. But, Secondly, the supposition on which you ground your argument is false. For white men, even Englishmen, are well able to labour in hot climates; provided they are temperate both in meat and drink, and that they inure themselves to it by degrees. I speak no more than I know by experience. It appears from the thermometer, that the summer heat in Georgia is frequently equal to that in Barbadoes, yea, to that under the line. And yet I and my family (eight in number) did employ all our spare time there, in felling of trees and clearing of ground, as hard labour as any Negro need be

employed in. The German family, likewise, forty in number, were employed in all manner of labour. And this was so far from impairing our health, that we all continued perfectly well, while the idle ones round about us were swept away as with a pestilence. It is not true, therefore, that white men are not able to labour, even in hot climates, full as well as black. But if they were not, it would be better that none should labour there, that the work should be left undone, than that myriads of innocent men should be murdered, and myriads more dragged into the basest slavery.

7. "But the furnishing us with slaves is necessary for the trade, and wealth, and glory of our nation." Here are several mistakes. For, First, wealth is not necessary to the glory of any nation; but wisdom, virtue, justice, mercy, generosity, public spirit, love of our country. These are necessary to the real glory of a nation; but abundance of wealth is not. Men of understanding allow that the glory of England was full as high in Queen Elizabeth's time as it is now; although our riches and trade were then as much smaller, as our virtue was greater. But, Secondly, it is not clear that we should have either less money or trade, (only less of that detestable trade of man-stealing,) if there was not a Negro in all our islands, or in all English America. It is demonstrable, white men, inured to it by degrees, can work as well as them; and they would do it, were Negroes out of the way, and proper encouragement given them. However, Thirdly, I come back to the same point: Better no trade, than trade procured by villany. It is far better to have no wealth, than to gain wealth at the expense of virtue. Better is honest poverty, than all the riches bought by the tears, and sweat, and blood, of our fellow-creatures.

8. "However this be, it is necessary, when we have slaves, to use them with severity." What, to whip them for every petty offence, till they are all in gore blood? to take that opportunity of rubbing pepper and salt into their raw flesh? to drop burning sealing-wax upon their skin? to castrate them? to cut off half their foot with an axe? to hang them on gibbets, that they may die by inches, with heat, and hunger, and thirst? to pin them down to the ground, and then burn them by degrees, from the

feet to the head? to roast them alive? When did a Turk or a Heathen find it necessary to use a fellow-creature thus?

I pray, to what end is this usage necessary? "Why, to prevent their running away; and to keep them constantly to their labour, that they may not idle away their time: So miserably stupid is this race of men, yea, so stubburn, and so wicked." Allowing them to be as stupid as you say, to whom is that stupidity owing? Without question, it lies altogether at the door of their inhuman masters; who give them no means, no opportunity, of improving their understanding; and, indeed, leave them no motive, either from hope or fear, to attempt any such thing. They were no way remarkable for stupidity while they remained in their own country: The inhabitants of Africa, where they have equal motives and equal means of improvement, are not inferior to the inhabitants of Europe; to some of them they are greatly superior. Impartially survey, in their own country, the natives of Benin, and the natives of Lapland; compare (setting prejudice aside) the Samoeids and the Angolans; and on which side does the advantage lie, in point of understanding? Certainly the African is in no respect inferior to the European. Their stupidity, therefore, in our plantations is not natural; otherwise than it is the natural effect of their condition. Consequently, it is not their fault, but yours: You must answer for it, before God and man.

9. "But their stupidity is not the only reason of our treating them with severity. For it is hard to say, which is the greatest, this, or their stubbornness and wickedness." It may be so: But do not these, as well as the other, lie at your door? Are not stubbornness, cunning, pilfering, and divers other vices, the natural, necessary fruits of slavery? Is not this an observation which has been made in every age and nation? And what means have you used to remove this stubbornness? Have you tried what mildness and gentleness would do? I knew one that did; that had prudence and patience to make the experiment; Mr. Hugh Bryan, who then lived on the borders of South Carolina. And what was the effect? Why, that all his Negroes (and he had no small number of them) loved and reverenced him as a father, and cheerfully obeyed him out of love. Yea,

they were more afraid of a frown from him, than of many blows from an overseer. And what pains have you taken, what method have you used, to reclaim them from their wickedness? Have you carefully taught them, that there is a God, a wise, powerful, merciful Being, the Creator and Governor of heaven and earth? that he has appointed a day wherein he will judge the world, will take an account of all our thoughts, words, and actions? that in that day he will reward every child of man according to his works? that then the righteous shall inherit the kingdom prepared for them from the foundation of the world; and the wicked shall be cast into everlasting fire, prepared for the devil and his angels? If you have not done this, if you have taken no pains or thought about the matter, can you wonder at their wickedness? What wonder, if they should cut your throat? And if they did, whom could you thank for it but yourself? You first acted the villain in making them slaves, whether you stole them or bought them. You kept them stupid and wicked, by cutting them off from all opportunities of improving either in knowledge or virtue: And now you assign their want of wisdom and goodness as the reason for using them worse than brute beasts!

V. 1. It remains only to make a little application of the preceding observations. But to whom should that application be made? That may bear a question. Should we address ourselves to the public at large? What effect can this have? It may inflame the world against the guilty, but is not likely to remove that guilt. Should we appeal to the English nation in general? This also is striking wide; and is never likely to procure any redress for the sore evil we complain of. As little would it in all probability avail, to apply to the Parliament. So many things, which seem of greater importance, lie before them, that they are not likely to attend to this. I therefore add a few words to those who are more immediately concerned, whether captains, merchants, or planters.

2. And, First, to the captains employed in this trade. Most of you know the country of Guinea; several parts of it, at least, between the river Senegal and the kingdom of Angola. Perhaps, now, by your means part of it is become a dreary, uncultivated

wilderness, the inhabitants being all murdered or carried away, so that there are none left to till the ground. But you well know how populous, how fruitful, how pleasant it was a few years ago. You know, the people were not stupid, not wanting in sense, considering the few means of improvement they enjoyed. Neither did you find them savage, fierce, cruel, treacherous, or unkind to strangers. On the contrary, they were, in most parts, a sensible and ingenious people. They were kind and friendly, courteous and obliging, and remarkably fair and just in their dealings. Such are the men whom you hire their own country-men to tear away from this lovely country; part by stealth, part by force, part made captives in those wars which you raise or foment on purpose. You have seen them torn away,—children from their parents, parents from their children; husbands from their wives, wives from their beloved husbands, brethren and sisters from each other. You have dragged them who had never done you any wrong, perhaps in chains, from their native shore. You have forced them into your ships like an herd of swine,— them who had souls immortal as your own; only some of them leaped into the sea, and resolutely stayed under water, till they could suffer no more from you. You have stowed them together as close as ever they could lie, without any regard either to decency or convenience. And when many of them had been poisoned by foul air, or had sunk under various hardships, you have seen their remains delivered to the deep, till the sea should give up his dead. You have carried the survivors into the vilest slavery, never to end but with life; such slavery as is not found among the Turks at Algiers, no, nor among the Heathens in America.

3. May I speak plainly to you? I must. Love constrains me; love to you, as well as to those you are concerned with.

Is there a God? You know there is. Is he a just God? Then there must be a state of retribution; a state wherein the just God will reward every man according to his works. Then what reward will he render to you? O think betimes! before you drop into eternity! Think now, "He shall have judgment without mercy that showed no mercy."

Are you a man? Then you should have an human heart. But

have you indeed? What is your heart made of? Is there no such principle as compassion there? Do you never feel another's pain? Have you no sympathy, no sense of human woe, no pity for the miserable? When you saw the flowing eyes, the heaving breasts, or the bleeding sides and tortured limbs of your fellow-creatures, was you a stone, or a brute? Did you look upon them with the eyes of a tiger? When you squeezed the agonizing creatures down in the ship, or when you threw their poor mangled remains into the sea, had you no relenting? Did not one tear drop from your eye, one sigh escape from your breast? Do you feel no relenting now? If you do not, you must go on, till the measure of your iniquities is full. Then will the great God deal with you as you have dealt with them, and require all their blood at your hands. And at "that day it shall be more tolerable for Sodom and Gomorrah than for you!" But if your heart does relent, though in a small degree, know it is a call from the God of love. And "to-day, if you will hear his voice, harden not your heart." To-day resolve, God being your helper, to escape for your life. Regard not money! All that a man hath will he give for his life! Whatever you lose, lose not your soul: Nothing can countervail that loss. Immediately quit the horrid trade: At all events, be an honest man.

4. This equally concerns every merchant who is engaged in the slave-trade. It is you that induce the African villain to sell his countrymen; and in order thereto, to steal, rob, murder men, women, and children without number, by enabling the English villain to pay him for so doing, whom you overpay for his execrable labour. It is your money that is the spring of all, that empowers him to go on: So that whatever he or the African does in this matter is all your act and deed. And is your conscience quite reconciled to this? Does it never reproach you at all? Has gold entirely blinded your eyes, and stupified your heart? Can you see, can you feel, no harm therein? Is it doing as you would be done to? Make the case your own. "Master," said a slave at Liverpool to the merchant that owned him, "what, if some of my countrymen were to come here, and take away my mistress, and Master Tommy, and Master Billy, and carry them into our country, and make them slaves, how

would you like it?" His answer was worthy of a man: "I will never buy a slave more while I live." O let his resolution be yours! Have no more any part in this detestable business. Instantly leave it to those unfeeling wretches who

Laugh at human nature and compassion!

Be you a man, not a wolf, a devourer of the human species! Be merciful, that you may obtain mercy!

5. And this equally concerns every gentleman that has an estate in our American plantations; yea, all slave-holders, of whatever rank and degree; seeing men-buyers are exactly on a level with men-stealers. Indeed you say, "I pay honestly for my goods; and I am not concerned to know how they are come by." Nay, but you are; you are deeply concerned to know they are honestly come by. Otherwise you are a partaker with a thief, and are not a jot honester than him. But you know they are not honestly come by; you know they are procured by means nothing near so innocent as picking of pockets, house-breaking, or robbery upon the highway. You know they are procured by a deliberate series of more complicated villany (of fraud, robbery, and murder) than was ever practised either by Mahometans or Pagans; in particular, by murders, of all kinds; by the blood of the innocent poured upon the ground like water. Now, it is your money that pays the merchant, and through him the captain and the African butchers. You therefore are guilty, yea, principally guilty, of all these frauds, robberies, and murders. You are the spring that puts all the rest in motion; they would not stir a step without you; therefore, the blood of all these wretches who die before their time, whether in their country or elsewhere, lies upon your head. "The blood of thy brother" (for, whether thou wilt believe it or no, such he is in the sight of Him that made him) "crieth against thee from the earth," from the ship, and from the waters. O, whatever it costs, put a stop to its cry before it be too late: Instantly, at any price, were it the half of your goods, deliver thyself from blood-guiltiness! Thy hands, thy bed, thy furniture, thy house, thy lands, are at present stained with blood. Surely it is enough; accumulate no more guilt; spill no

more the blood of the innocent! Do not hire another to shed blood; do not pay him for doing it! Whether you are a Christian or no, show youself a man! Be no more savage than a lion or a bear!

6. Perhaps you will say, "I do not buy any Negroes; I only use those left me by my father." So far is well; but is it enough to satisfy your own conscience? Had your father, have you, has any man living, a right to use another as a slave? It cannot be, even setting Revelation aside. It cannot be, that either war, or contract, can give any man such a property in another as he has in his sheep and oxen. Much less is it possible, that any child of man should ever be born a slave. Liberty is the right of every human creature, as soon as he breathes the vital air; and no human law can deprive him of that right which he derives from the law of nature.

If, therefore, you have any regard to justice, (to say nothing of mercy, nor the revealed law of God,) render unto all their due. Give liberty to whom liberty is due, that is, to every child of man, to every partaker of human nature. Let none serve you but by his own act and deed, by his own voluntary choice. Away with all whips, all chains, all compulsion! Be gentle toward all men; and see that you invariably do unto every one as you would he should do unto you.

7. O thou God of love, thou who art loving to every man, and whose mercy is over all thy works; thou who art the Father of the spirits of all flesh, and who art rich in mercy unto all; thou who hast mingled of one blood all the nations upon earth; have compassion upon these outcasts of men, who are trodden down as dung upon the earth! Arise, and help these that have no helper, whose blood is spilt upon the ground like water! Are not these also the work of thine own hands, the purchase of thy Son's blood? Stir them up to cry unto thee in the land of their captivity; and let their complaint come up before thee; let it enter into thy ears! Make even those that lead them away captive to pity them, and turn their captivity as the rivers in the south. O burst thou all their chains in sunder; more especially the chains of their sins! Thou Saviour of all, make them free, that they may be free indeed!

James Ramsay, On the Treatment and Conversion of African Slaves, 1784

Objections to African Capacity, drawn from Observation, considered.

The ingenious author of a late History of Jamaica, has treated this subject at considerable length, and appears to have formed, from his own observation, the same opinion as Hume's, of negroes being a distinct race. To suppose them only a distinct race, will not immediately affect our arguments for their humane treatment and mental improvement; but the consequences usually drawn from it shock humanity, and check every hope of their advancement: for, if allowed to be a *distinct* race, European pride immediately concludes them an *inferior* race, and then it follows, of course, that nature formed them to be slaves to their superiors. And the master having established these premises generally, and complimented himself with a place among the superior beings, fairly concludes himself loosed from all obligations, but those of interest, in his conduct towards them. A horse and a bull, are animals each of a different species, but the superiority has not been established between them, nor the inferior brought into bondage by the lordly master. For argument's sake, suppose negroes of a different and even of an inferior race, still, we know they are capable of forming, and actually have formed, free independent societies; and, though they have not yet attained the refinements and luxuries of Europe, yet have they shewn no small ingenuity in compacting themselves together, and made no mean progress in many of the arts of life. And to help to compose, and be a member of a free state, is more honourable, and gives greater scope to the mental powers, than to be the most polished slave in America or Europe. Still, being such, are they to be dragged away from a country adapted to their constitutions, from plenty of nutritious food, to which they have been accustomed from infancy, to work as slaves, hungry, naked, torn with stripes, in a distant, unfavourable clime, for the avarice and lusts of, perhaps, some of the most worthless persons of the pretendedly superior families, with whom they had neither acquaintance or connection? Suppose different races, and that they vary in point of excellence; yet, in what chapter of nature's law is it declared, that one quarter of the globe shall breed slaves for the rest? Where shall we find a charter conferring authority on the one, and ascertaining the submission of the other? Are no conditions annexed, no rights reserved, which, when violated, the subjected race can plead before their common Lord? Such a state cannot be imagined as existing under the government of God: it is blasphemy against his benevolence even to suppose it. The inanimate and brute creation was fitted for and submitted to man's dominion; but man himself was left independent of every personal claim in his fellows. And nothing but an implied voluntary surrender of his independency to society, for the benefits of law, can controul or lessen his claim. But North-American or West-Indian slavery implies no surrender, supposes no submission, but to necessity and force.

Had nature intended negroes for slavery, she would have endowed them with many qualities which they now want. Their food would have needed no preparation, their bodies no covering; they would have been born without any sentiment for liberty; and, possessing a patience not to be provoked, would have been incapable of resentment or opposition; that high treason against the divine right of European dominion. A horse or a cow, when abused, beaten, or starved, will try to get out of the reach of the lash, and make no scruple of attempting the nearest inclosure to get at pasture. But we have not heard of their withdrawing themselves from the service of an hard master, nor of avenging with his blood the cruelty of his treatment.

To suppose different, especially superior and inferior races, supposes different rules of conduct, and a different line of duty necessary to be prescribed for them. But where do we find traces of this difference in the present case? Vice never appeared in Africa in a more barbarous and shocking garb, than she is seen every day in the most polished parts of Europe. Europe has not shewn greater elevation of sentiment than has shone through the gloom of Africa. We can see cause why the nations, into which for the purposes of society mankind has been divided, should have characteristic marks of complexion and features, (and almost the whole of the present subject of discussion may be resolved into these) to tie, by the resemblance, fellow-citizens more closely and affectionately together. And, be it remarked, that these signs are mere arbitrary impressions, that neither give nor take away animal or rational powers; but, in their effect, are confined to the purpose for which they appear to have been impressed, the binding of tribes and families together. Farther, climate, mode of living, and accidental prevalence of particular customs, will account for many national characteristics.

But the soul is a simple substance, not to be distinguished by squat or tall, black, brown, or fair. Hence all the difference that can take place in it is a greater or less degree of energy, a more or less complete correspondence of action, with the circumstances in which the agent is placed. In short, we can have no idea of intellect, but as acting with infinite power and perfect propriety in the Deity, and with various degrees of limited power and propriety, in the several orders of intelligent created beings; so that there is nothing to distinguish these several created orders, but more or less power; and nothing to hinder us from supposing the possible gradual advancement of the lower into the higher ranks of created beings. But we cannot, in like manner, speak of the change of a bull into an horse, or of a swine into an elephant. The annihilation of the one is included in the transmutation into the other, because in it that is lost which constituted the specific difference.

We can plainly see the propriety of different pursuits, and different degrees of exertion of the reasoning energetic powers in the several individuals that compose a community, for carrying on the various purposes of society. But there is not, therefore, a necessity to have recourse to different species of souls, as if the peasant had one sort, the mechanic a second, the man of learning a third; yet whatever concludes for the propriety of races differing in point of excellence, will conclude also for a difference in these. And we see, in contradiction to all such reveries, that communities flourish in proportion as the less of any other difference takes place, than that in which society naturally disposeth of its members for their mutual or joint benefit. The soul is versatile, and being simple in itself takes its manner and tincture from the objects around it; it universally appears to be fitted only for that character in which it is to act: but that this is not an indelible character appears plainly in every page of the history of mankind. Look into our books of travels, and, in persons no ways remarkable for genius or invention, admire the almost incredible efforts and productions of necessity. How often has the shepherd shone out as a statesman, and the peasant triumphed as a general? Can we suppose greater difference between the African and European, than, for example, between the keeper of sheep, and the Governor of men; between leading an herd of gregarious animals out to pasture, and directing the complicated genius and bent of that various creature man, either to counteract or attain the purposes of society: yet the only difference between them lies in the direction given to the mental faculties.

Thus far we have opposed opinion with argument, and, excepting a remark of which we shall take notice, we may leave all that the author above-mentioned has advanced of the inferiority of negroes, to be contrasted with the instances given by himself of their energy, abilities, and sentiment, and to be compared with the instances of stupidity to be found in the most polished nations. For, as we have proved, if we establish the notion of different races, we must still draw a line between the highest of the one, and the lowest of that next above it. Particularly, we may say of his example, Francis Williams the negroe poet and mathematician, that though his verses bear no great marks of genius, yet, there have been bred at the same university an hundred white masters of arts, and many doctors, who could not improve them; and, therefore, his particular success in the fields of science cannot operate against the natural abilities of those of his colour, till it be proved, that every white man bred there has outstripped him. But allowance is to be made for his being a solitary essay, and the possibility of a wrong choice having been made in him. Childish sprightliness, for which it seems he was singled out ior the trial, is not always, nor indeed often, a faithful promiser of manly parts; too frequently it withers without fruit, like the early blossoms of the spring. Other gentlemen of Jamaica speak highly of his abilities, and of the favour they procured for him.

Thomas Clarkson, On the Slavery and Commerce of the Human Species, 1786

We come now to that other system of reasoning, which is always applied, when the former is confuted; "that the Africans are an inferiour link of the chain of nature, and are made for slavery."

This assertion is proved by two arguments; the first of which was advanced also by the ancients, and is drawn from the *inferiority of their capacities*.

Let us allow then for a moment, that they appear to have no parts, that they appear to be void of understanding. And is this wonderful, when you *receivers* depress their senses by hunger? Is this wonderful, when by incessant labour, the continual application of the lash, and the most inhuman treatment that imagination can devise, you overwhelm their genius, and hinder it from breaking forth?—No,—You confound their abilities by the severity of their servitude: for as a spark of fire, if crushed by too great a weight of incumbent fuel, cannot be blown into a flame, but suddenly expires, so the human mind, if depressed by rigorous servitude, cannot be excited to a display of those faculties, which might otherwise have shone with the brightest lustre.

Neither is it wonderful in another point of view. For what is it that awakens the abilities of men, and distinguishes them from the common herd? Is it not often the amiable hope of becoming serviceable to individuals, or the state? Is it not often the hope of riches, or of power? Is it not frequently the hope of temporary honours, or a lasting fame? These principles have all a wonderful effect upon the mind. They call upon it to exert its faculties, and bring those talents to the publick view, which had otherwise been concealed. But the unfortunate Africans have no such incitements as these, that they should shew their genius. They have no hope of riches, power, honours, fame. They have no hope but this, that their miseries will be soon terminated by death.

And here we cannot but censure and expose the murmurings of the unthinking and the gay; who, going on in a continual round of pleasure and prosperity, repine at the will of Providence, as exhibited in the shortness of human duration. But let a weak and infirm old age overtake them: let them experience calamities: let them feel but half the miseries which the wretched Africans undergo, and they will praise the goodness of Providence, who hath made them mortal; who hath prescribed certain ordinary bounds to the life of man; and who, by such a limitation, hath given all men this comfortable hope, that however persecuted in life, a time will come, in the common course of nature, when their sufferings will have an end.

Such then is the nature of this servitude, that we can hardly expect to find in those, who undergo it, even the glimpse of genius. For if their minds are in a continual state of depression, and if they have no expectations in life to awaken their abilities, and make them eminent, we cannot be surprized if a sullen gloomy stupidity should be the leading mark in their character; or if they should appear inferiour to those, who do not only enjoy the invaluable blessings of freedom, but have every prospect before their eyes, that can allure them to exert their faculties. Now, if to these considerations we add, that the wretched Africans are torn from their country in a state of nature, and that in general, as long as their slavery continues, every obstacle is placed in the way of their improvement, we shall have a sufficient answer to any argument that may be drawn from the inferiority of their capacities.

It appears then, from the circumstances that have been mentioned, that to form a true judgment of the abilities of these unfortunate people, we must either take a general view of them before their slavery commences, or confine our attention to such, as, after it has commenced, have had any opportunity given them of shewing their genius either in arts or letters. If, upon such a fair and impartial view, there should be any reason to suppose, that they are at all inferiour to others in the same situation, the argument will then gain some of that weight and importance, which it wants at present.

In their own country, where we are to see them first, we must expect that the prospect will be unfavourable. They are mostly in a savage state. Their powers of mind are limited to few objects. Their ideas are consequently few. It appears, however, that they follow the same mode of life, and exercise the same arts, as the ancestors of those very Europeans, who boast of their great superiority, are described to have done in the same uncultivated state. This appears from the Nubian's Geography, the writings of Leo, the Moor, and all the subsequent histories, which those, who have visited the African continent, have written from their own inspection. Hence three conclusions; that their abilities are sufficient for their situation; —that they are as great, as those of other people have been, in the same stage of society;—and that they are as great as those of any civilized people whatever, when the degree of the barbarism of the one is drawn into a comparison with that of the civilization of the other.

Let us now follow them to the colonies. They are carried over in the unfavourable situation described. It is observed here, that though their abilities cannot be estimated high from a want of cultivation, they are yet various, and that they vary in proportion as the nation, from which they have been brought, has advanced more or less in the scale of social life. This observation, which is so frequently made, is of great importance: for if their abilities expand in porportion to the improvement of their state, it is a clear indication, that if they were equally improved, they would be equally ingenious.

But here, before we consider any opportunities that may be afforded them, let it be remembered that even their most polished situation may be called barbarous, and that this circumstance, should they appear less docile than others, may be considered as a sufficient answer to any objection that may be made to their capacities. Notwithstanding this, when they are put to the mechanical arts, they do not discover a want of ingenuity. They attain them in as short a time as the Europeans, and arrive at a degree of excellence equal to that of their teachers. This is a fact, almost universally known, and affords us this proof, that having learned with facility such of the mechanical arts, as they have been taught, they are capable of attaining any other, at least, of the same class, if they should receive but the same instruction.

With respect to the liberal arts, their proficiency is certainly less; but not less in proportion to their time and opportunity of study; not less, because they are less capable of attaining them, but because they have seldom or ever an opportunity of learning them at all. It is yet extraordinary that their talents appear, even in some of these sciences, in which they are totally uninstructed. Their abilities in musick are such, as to have been generally noticed. They play frequently upon a variety of instruments, without any other assistance than their own ingenuity. They have also tunes of their own composition. Some of these have been imported among us; are now in use; and are admired for their sprightliness and ease, though the ungenerous and prejudiced importer has concealed their original.

Neither are their talents in poetry less conspicuous. Every occurrence, if their spirits are not too greatly depressed, is turned into a song. These songs are said to be incoherent and nonsensical. But this proceeds principally from two causes, an improper conjunction of words, arising from an ignorance of the language in which they compose; and a wildness of thought, arising from the different manner, in which the organs of rude and civilized people will be struck by the same object. And as to their want of harmony and rhyme, which is the last objection, the difference of pronunciation is the cause. Upon the whole, as they are perfectly consistent with their own ideas, and are strictly musical as pronounced by themselves, they afford us as high a proof of their poetical powers, as the works of the most acknowledged poets.

The second argument, by which it is attempted to be proved, "that the Africans are an inferiour link of the chain of nature, and are designed for slavery," is drawn from *colour*, and from those other marks, which distinguish them from the inhabitants of Europe.

To prove this with the greater facility, the *receivers* divide in opinion. Some of them contend that the Africans, from these circumstances, are the descendants of Cain: others, that they are the posterity of Ham; and that as it was declared by divine inspiration, that these should be servants to the rest of the world, so they are designed for slavery; and that the reducing of them to such a situation is only the accomplishment of the will of heaven: while the rest, considering them from the same circumstances as a totally distinct species of men, conclude them to be an inferiour link of the chain of nature, and deduce the inference described.

If then the scriptures are true, it is evident that the posterity of Cain were extinguished in the flood. Thus one of the arguments is no more.

With respect to the curse of Ham, it appears also that it was limited; that it did not extend to the posterity of all his sons, but only to the descendants of him who was called Canaan: by which it was foretold that the Canaanites, a part of the posterity of Ham, should serve the posterity of Shem and Japhet. Now how does it appear that these wretched Africans are the descendants of Canaan?—By those marks, it will be said, which distinguish them from the rest of the world.—But where are these marks to be found in the divine writings? In what page is it said, that the Canaanites were to be known by their *colour*, their *features*, their *form*, or the very *hair of their heads*, which is brought into the account?—But alas! so far are the divine writings from giving any such account, that they shew the assertion to be false. They shew that the descendants of Cush were of the colour, to which the advocates for slavery allude; and of course, that there was no such limitation of colour to the posterity of Canaan, or the inheritors of the curse.

Suppose we should now shew, upon the most undeniable evidence, that those of the wretched Africans, who are singled out as inheriting the curse, are the descendants of Cush or Phut; and that we should shew farther, that but a single remnant of Canaan, which was afterwards ruined, was ever in Africa at all.—Here all is consternation.—

But unfortunately again for the argument, though wonderfully for the confirmation that the scriptures are of divine original, the whole prophecy has been completed. A part of the descendants of Canaan were hewers of wood and drawers of water, and became tributary and subject to the Israelites, or the descendants of Shem. The Greeks afterwards, as well as the Romans, who were both the descendants of Japhet, not only subdued those who were settled in Syria and Palestine, but pursued and conquered all such as were then remaining. These were the Tyrians and Carthaginians: the former of whom were ruined by Alexander and the Greeks, the latter by Scipio and the Romans.

It appears then that the second argument is wholly inapplicable and false: that it is false in its *application*, because those, who were the objects of the curse, were a totally distinct people: that it is false in its *proof*, because no such distinguishing marks, as have been specified, are to be found in the divine writings: and that, if the proof could be made out, it would be now *inapplicable*, as the curse has been long completed.

From these, and the whole of the preceding observations on the subject, we may conclude, that as all the inhabitants of the earth cannot be otherwise than the children of the same parents, and as the difference of their appearance must have of course proceeded from incidental causes, these causes are a combination of those qualities, which we call *climate*; that the blackness of the *Africans* is so far ingrafted in their constitution, in a course of many generations, that their children wholly inherit it, if brought up in the same spot, but that it is not so absolutely interwoven in their nature, that it cannot be removed, if they are born and settled in another; that *Noah* and his sons were probably of an *olive* complexion; that those of their descendants, who went farther to the south, became of a deeper olive or *copper*; while those, who went still farther, became of a deeper copper or *black*; that those, on the other hand, who travelled farther to the north, became less olive or *brown*, while those who went still farther than the former, became less brown or *white*; and that if any man were to point out any one of the colours which prevails in the human complexion, as likely to furnish an argument, that the people of such a complexion were of a different species from the rest, it is probable that his own descendants, if removed to the climate to which this complexion is peculiar, would, in the course of a few generations, degenerate into the same colour.

Having now replied to the argument, "that the Africans are an inferiour link of the chain of nature," as far as it depended on their *capacity* and *colour*, we shall now only take notice of an expression, which the *receivers* before-mentioned are pleased to make use of, "that they are made for slavery."

Had the Africans been *made for slavery*, or to become the property of any society of men, it is clear, from the observations that have been made in the second part of this Essay, that they must have been created *devoid of reason*: but this is contrary to fact. It is clear also, that there must have been many and evident signs of the *inferiority of their nature*, and that this society of men must have had a *natural right* to their dominion: but this is equally false. No such signs of *inferiority* are to be found in the one, and the right to dominion in the other is *incidental*: for in what volume of nature or religion is it written, that one society of men should *breed slaves* for the benefit of another? Nor is it less evident that they would have wanted many of those qualities which they have, and which brutes have not: they would have wanted that *spirit of liberty*, that *sense of ignominy and shame*, which so frequently drives them to the horrid extremity of finishing their own existence. Nor would they have been endowed with a *contemplative power*; for such a power would have been unnecessary to people in such a situation; or rather, its only use could have been to increase their pain. We cannot suppose therefore that God has made an order of beings, with such mental qualities and powers, for the sole purpose of being used as *beasts*, or *instruments* of labour. And here, what a dreadful argument presents itself against you *receivers*? For if they have no understandings as you confess, then is your conduct impious, because, as they cannot perceive the intention of your punishment, your severities cannot make them better. But if, on the other hand, they have had under-standings, (which has evidently appeared) then is your conduct equally impious, who, by destroying their faculties by the severity of your discipline, have reduced men, who had once the power of reason, to an equality with the brute creation.

William Dickson, Letter on Slavery, 1789

I call colour (the principal difference in the varieties of men) a very equivocal mark of superiority. I cannot tell, Sir, what passes in the minds of other men; but, in my own mind, I never could perceive any connection whatsoever between my idea of *intellect*, and my idea of *colour*. The white man reasons thus, The negro's *colour* is different from mine, *ergo* I am naturally *superior* to the negro. May not a copper-coloured man, or an olive-coloured man, or a tawney man, or a *black* man thus demonstrate the natural superiority of men of his *own* colour, to all others? By such sort of logic, we find the celebrated Francis Williams attempting to demonstrate the superiority of the negro to the mulatto: 'A simple white or a simple black complexion was respectively perfect; but a mulatto, being a heterogeneous medley of both, was *imperfect*, *ergo inferior*.' I suspect, Sir, that the ideas of intellect and of colour have a mutual dependence in minds which pretend to be superior to that of our black philosopher.—The whites paint the devil black, and the negroes paint him white; but do such chimeras prove the devil to be either black or white? A man may associate his idea of *blackness* with his idea of the devil, or with his idea of *stupidity*, or with any other of his ideas he thinks proper; but he ought not to reason from such arbitrary associations.

. . . Again, if it be just to affirm that the blackest and the fairest nations had different origins, may not the same be as justly affirmed of those of the intermediate shades of colour? Must we not, then, conclude that the swarthy Spaniard and the fair German or Pole are descended from two original human pairs, of their respective complexions? At this rate, we shall have Adams and Eves without number—one pair, at least, for every country. The difficulty will be to find gardens of Eden in some countries, in Labrador, for example, or Lapland, or Kamtschatka.

. . . Upon the whole, Sir, I am, by no means, singular in thinking, That as difference of soil and culture give rise to many varieties of vegetables, those of the potatoe, for example, or the apple; and as very considerable changes are known to be produced on some species of animals, as dogs, horses, sheep, &c. by domestication, climate, and other causes; so the varieties of the human species may be produced by the *slow* but *long continued* and combined operation of soil, climate and mode of living—by *physical* joined with *moral* causes.

This opinion . . . I shall reinforce with an observation of one of the greatest physiologists in Europe: That most animals in their wild state are of a dark colour; and that, when domesticated, they generally assume a lighter hue, and often become perfectly white. Of this we have very striking examples in the duck, the goose, the dunghill fowl, the pigeon, the turkey, the cat, and others, perhaps, which may occur to gentlemen skilled in natural history. Let the apologists for slavery beware, lest they stir up naturalists to investigate this matter with redoubled ardour; for it seems not improbable that the result of their inquiries may be, That the negroes are the aborigines of mankind.

It has been suggested That the negro occupies a place in the scale of being, or forms a link in that chain which connects the white man with the Orang Outang; but, here, Sir, is a chasm, which it is impossible for any *one* link to fill up; and, I am apt to think that the modern manufacturers of systems will have hard work to forge links sufficient in strength and number to connect creatures so widely distant as a human being and a Kakurlacko. The external resemblance, however, in figure and motion of some of the monkey tribes, to mankind, is a striking and a mortifying resemblance. This circumstance it is, which misleads superficial observers; for their moral structure is totally different from that of mankind. Indocile, speechless, and, consequently destitute of the power of abstraction and the moral and religious sense, in real and useful sagacity, they fall

G

much behind the dog and the horse, not to mention what we have been told, of the 'half-reasoning elephant.' The Creator, when he wisely allotted to every animal that portion of those mysterious faculties, instinct and sagacity, which was most proper for their condition, seems not to have impressed, on any being, inferior to man, the least signature of himself. Accordingly some philosophers chuse to characterize mankind by the religious sense, rather than by reason, the former being, in their opinion, the most unequivocal criterion of his nature. 'And God said, Let us make man *in our image,*' is the decision of revelation. Now it is certain, That the negroes have a just sense of right and wrong, and make the common moral distinctions, with much acuteness and accuracy.—They may even be said to 'draw a hasty moral—a sudden sense of right.'—If they do not, I ask *with what* JUSTICE *the pretended, superior race of men inflict on them* EXEMPLARY *punishments, and, sometimes, doom them to expire by horrible tortures?*

... I have endeavoured to answer the preceding arguments, in the sense in which, I know, they are taken by the vulgar, in the West Indies; and in which, I suspect, they are understood by persons who rank themselves far above the vulgar, not in the West Indies only, but even in this country. Those reasoners infer natural inferiority from the peculiar colour and features of the Africans, *immediately,* or without interposing any connecting idea. Other defenders of this system, if I rightly understand them, state the argument thus. 'The external peculiarities of the negroes are so many specific differences. The negroes, then, are a species of men different from, and therefore, inferior to the whites.' But, by what logic can inferiority be deduced from difference of species, supposing it proved, any more than from the pretended specific differences? And, is it more agreeable to philosophy and to common sense to say, He is of a *different,* and, therefore, an *inferior* species of men, than to affirm, That he has a *black skin,* and is, therefore, *inferior?*— Some men may suppose it their interest to cherish such vulgar errors; but it is the business of philosophy to explode them; especially when, as in the present instance, they are evidently repugnant to the happiness of mankind.

It cannot be denied that the negroes, when put to a trade which happens to coincide with the bent of their genius, become as good, and, sometimes, better artificers, than white men. I have seen a white carpenter drudging with the saw, jacking-plane, &c. and who could not lay off his work properly, while a black one was employed in making pannel-doors, sash-windows, &c. I have known the carpenter's work of a good house of two stories, with a pavilion-roof, king-posts, &c. planned and conducted, by a black carpenter—On the doors of some of the negro huts, I have observed wooden locks, at once simple and well contrived, and which it was impossible to open, without the wooden key, which had two or three square, polished prominencies, adapted to the internal parts of the lock, which I have also seen, but it cannot be explained without a model.—In the learned Dr. Burney's History of Music, there are figures of several ancient musical instruments, by a comparison with which, the banjay or coromantin drum would lose nothing. This last is a most ear-piercing instrument; but, being prohibited, is but seldom used, by the negroes, in Barbadoes. The black musicians, however, have substituted, in its place, a common earthen jar, on beating the aperture of which, with the extended palms of their hands, it emits a hollow sound, resembling the more animating note of the drum.—As silver-smiths and watch-makers, the negroes shew no want of genius. I have employed a black watch-maker who was instructed in the art, by a most ingenious mechanic and natural philosopher, in Bridgetown. That worthy person (now deceased) was bred a mathematical instrument maker, in London; and I knew him to be a person of too strict probity to have put people's watches into improper hands.—But, without enumerating such instances, I might, at once, have appealed, for a proof of African ingenuity, to the fabric and colours of the Guinea cloths, which most people must have seen.—By the word *mechanic* is generally meant a person who makes but little use of his rational faculty; but it must be remembered that *mechanical contrivance* is one of the highest departments of reason. Nor can this be otherwise; since, the science of mechanics depends entirely on mathematics, and

G*

hath exercised the genius of an Archimedes, of a Galilæo, of an Emerson, of a M'Laurin, and, above all, of that great ornament of this island, and of the human species, the immortal *Newton*.

The fondness of the negroes for music, and the proficiency they sometimes make in it, with little or no instruction, is too well known to need support, from particular instances. This their taste for melody and harmony, if it does not demonstrate their rationality, ought, at least, to be admitted as an argument in proving their *humanity*.

. . . On the supposition that the negroes are not moral agents, co-ordinate with the whites, I asked with what *justice*, and I might have asked with what *sense*, the pretended superior race inflict on them *exemplary* punishments, and, sometimes, doom them to expire, by horrible tortures?—Those who direct the labours of cattle stimulate them to exertion by stripes. Dogs, being more sagacious, are punished, by the huntsman and the shepherd, with more severity, and with some little view to improvement. Every needless stripe, however, even on dogs or horses or asses, is accounted a mark of the inflictor's barbarous disposition. But no person thinks of inflicting *exemplary* punishments on *brutes*.

But, although it could be proved that the understandings of the Africans are weaker than those of the Europeans, it will, by no means, follow that the latter have a right to enslave them; since, on this principle, no such thing as national liberty could ever have existed in the world. And it may be asked what would become of the liberties of the lower orders even of Britons, were their title to those liberties to depend on powers of reason or of imagination, which bore but a small proportion to those of the great men who have done honour to this island and to mankind?

Let the Europeans be superior in *reason*. Ought they not also to be superior in point of *justice* and *mercy?* And are they superior in justice, and mercy?—Let the Africans tell!

But, setting aside reason altogether, the *passions* of the negroes prove that they were not created to be slaves; any more than the fierce lion was created to 'abide by a master's crib, or to harrow the vallies after him,' which appears to have been the destination of the horse and the ox. Those who complain of the passionate *vindictive* tempers of the Africans cannot surely be aware that they are demonstrating the utter repugnancy of slavery to their nature. That a creature should have been *formed* for a state which he *abhors*, is an exception to the general œconomy of the universe. That beings created for slavery, should be endowed with stubborn, rebellious, unconquerable passions which spurn the yoke, and often prove fatal both to themselves and to their lords, is a paradox which we leave those of their lords who believe it, to explain, by the newly broached theories of slavery. The theories of scepticism, which have helped them out, on other occasions, will assist them on this.—It would be strange indeed, if there were not a close analogy, a certain sympathetic affinity, between the paradoxes of slavery and those of infidelity!

William Wilberforce, An Appeal in behalf of the Negro Slaves, 1823

I press these topics the more earnestly, because there has prevailed among many of our statesmen, of late years, a most unwarrantable and pernicious disposition to leave all that concerns the well-being of the slaves to the colonial legislatures. Surely this is a course manifestly contrary to the clearest obligations of duty. The very relation in which the Negro slaves and the members of the colonial assemblies, which consist wholly of their masters, stand towards each other, is of itself a decisive reason why the imperial legislature ought to consider itself bound to exercise the office of an umpire, or rather of a judge between them, as constituting two parties of conflicting interests and feelings. And this, let it be remembered, not merely because, knowing the frailty of our common nature, and its disposition to abuse absolute power, we ought not to deliver the weaker party altogether into the power of the stronger; but because in the present instance there are peculiar objections of great force, some of which have been already noticed. In truth, West Indians must be exempt from the ordinary frailties of human nature, if, living continually with those wretched beings, and witnessing their extreme degradation and consequent depravity, they could entertain for the Negroes, in an unimpaired degree, that equitable consideration and that fellow-feeling, which are due from man to man; so as to sympathise properly with them in their sufferings and wrongs, or form a just estimate of their claims to personal rights and moral improvement.

The fact is, that though the old prejudice, that the Negroes are creatures of an inferior nature, is no longer maintained in terms, there is yet too much reason to fear that a latent impression arising from it still continues practically to operate in the colonies, and to influence the minds of those who have the government of the slaves, in estimating their physical claims, and still more those of their moral nature. The colonists, indeed, and the abolitionists, would differ as to facts, in speaking of the sufficiency of the slave's supply of food, and of his treatment in some other particulars. But on what other principle than that of the inferiority of the species, can it be explained, that, in estimating what is due to the Negroes, all consideration of their moral nature has been altogether left out? When it is undeniable that they have no more power of giving their testimony against any white ruffian by whom they may have been maltreated, than if they were of the brute creation; that they are worked like cattle under the whip; that they are strangers to the institution of marriage, and to all the blessed truths of Christianity; how, but from their supposed inferiority of nature, could we nevertheless be assured by the colonial legislatures, with the most unhesitating confidence, that whatever defects there might formerly have been in their treatment, they are now as well used *as can reasonably be desired?* If such be indeed their opinion, whether that opinion proceeds from the views here intimated or not, it would still suffice to show the criminality, of our committing to them the destiny of the slaves. For let it be observed, there is not in this instance any difference as to the facts of the case; nor do the colonists affirm what we deny, as to the moral degradation of the slaves. Both parties, for instance, agree that promiscuous intercourse between the sexes, and Pagan darkness, are nearly universal among them; and yet the colonists contend that the slaves are as well treated and governed as they need to be. Can then the members of the British Parliament conscientiously devolve the duty of establishing such religious and moral reforms, as I trust it must be the universal wish of every member of the empire to introduce among the Negroes, upon those, who, to say nothing of the extremity of personal degradation, consider marriage and Christianity as unworthy of their regard, in estimating the condition of their fellow creatures?

Indeed, the West Indians, in the warmth of argument, have gone still farther, and have even distinctly told us, again and again, and I am shocked to say that some of their partizans in this country have re-echoed the assertion, that these poor degraded beings, the Negro slaves, are as well or even better off than our British peasantry,—a proposition so monstrous, that nothing can possibly exhibit in a stronger light the extreme force of the prejudices which must exist in the minds of its assertors. A Briton to compare the state of a West Indian slave with that of an English freeman, and to give the former the preference! It is to imply an utter insensibility of the native feelings and moral dignity of man, no less than of the rights of Englishmen!! I will not condescend to argue this question, as I might, on the ground of comparative feeding and clothing, and lodging, and medical attendance. Are these the only claims? are these the chief privileges of a rational and immortal being? Is the consciousness of personal independence nothing? are self-possession and self-government nothing? Is it of no account that our persons are inviolate by any private authority, and that the whip is placed only in the hands of the public executioner; Is it of no value that we have the power of pursuing the occupation and the habits of life which we prefer; that we have the prospect, or at least the hope, of improving our condition, and of rising, as we have seen others rise, from poverty and obscurity to comfort, and opulence, and distinction? Again, are all the charities of the heart, which arise out of the domestic relations, to be considered as nothing; and, I may add, all their security too among men who are free agents, and not vendible

chattels, liable continually to be torn from their dearest connections, and sent into a perpetual exile? Are husband and
wife, parent and child, terms of no meaning? Are willing
services, or grateful returns for voluntary kindnesses, nothing?
But, above all, is Christianity so little esteemed among us, that
we are to account as of no value the hope, "full of immortality,"
the light of heavenly truth, and all the consolations and
supports by which religion cheers the hearts and elevates the
principles, and dignifies the conduct of multitudes of our
labouring classes in this free and enlightened country? Is it
nothing to be taught that all human distinctions will soon be
at an end; that all the labours and sorrows of poverty and
hardship will soon exist no more; and to know, on the express
authority of Scripture, that the lower classes, instead of being
an inferior order in the creation, are even the preferable objects
of the love of the Almighty?

But such wretched sophisms as insult the understandings of
mankind, are sometimes best answered by an appeal to their
feelings. Let me therefore ask, is there, in the whole of the three
kingdoms, a parent or a husband so sordid and insensible that
any sum, which the richest West Indian proprietor could offer
him, would be deemed a compensation for his suffering his
wife or his daughter to be subjected to the brutal outrage of the
cart-whip—to the savage lust of the driver—to the indecent,
and degrading, and merciless punishment of a West Indian
whipping? If there were one so dead, I say not to every liberal,
but to every natural feeling, as that money could purchase of
him such concessions, such a wretch, and he alone, would be
capable of the farther sacrifices necessary for degrading an
English peasant to the condition of a West Indian slave. He
might consent to sell the liberty of his own children, and to
barter away even the blessings conferred on himself by that
religion which declares to him that his master, no less than
himself, has a Master in heaven—a common Creator, who is
no respecter of persons, and in whose presence he may weekly
stand on the same spiritual level with his superiors in rank, to
be reminded of their common origin, common responsibility,
and common day of final and irreversible account. . . .

The information also which we now possess, as to the African character, would aggravate our criminality. For though the day, I trust, is gone by for ever, in which the alleged inferiority of intellect and incurable barbarity of the African race were supposed to extenuate their oppression, yet it ought not to be left unnoticed, that the notions which formerly prevailed to their prejudice, in these respects, have of late years been abundantly refuted, not only by authority but experience. It may be confidently affirmed, that there never was any un-civilised people of whose dispositions we have received a more amiable character than that which is given of the native Africans by Parke and Golberry, both of whom visited those districts of Africa from which victims for the Slave Trade were furnished; and whose testimony in their favour will naturally be admitted with less reserve, because neither of them could be biassed by any wish to discountenance the Slave Trade, they having evidently felt no desire for its abolition.

But it is at Sierra Leone, that long despised and calumniated colony, that the African character has been most effectually and experimentally vindicated. The first seeds of civilization which were sown there by the Christian philanthropy of Mr. Granville Sharpe nearly perished from the unkindly soil to which they had been committed, but they were saved from early destruction, and cultured at length successfully, under the fostering care and indefatigable attention of the late excellent Mr. H. Thornton, and by other good and able men, who, both at home and in the colony, co-operated with him; by one living benefactor especially, who will be hereafter venerated as the steady, enlightened, and unwearied, though unostentatious friend of Africa. It is at Sierra Leone that the great experiment on human nature has been tried; and there it has appeared, that the poor African barbarians, just rescued from the holds of slave-ships, are capable, not merely of being civilized, but of soon enjoying, with advantage, the rights and institutions of British freemen. In truth, to have formed any conclusions against the Negroes from the experience we had of them in their state of bondage, was not less unphilosophical than unjust. It was remarked by M. Dupuis, the British consul at Mogadore, that even the generality of European Christians, after a long captivity and severe treatment among the Arabs, appeared at first exceedingly stupid and insensible. "If," he adds, "they have been any considerable time in slavery, they appear lost to reason and feeling; their spirits broken, and their faculties sunk in a species of stupor, which I am unable adequately to describe. They appear degraded even below the Negro slave. The succession of hardships, without any protecting law to which they can appeal for any alleviation or redress, seems to destroy every spring of exertion or hope in their minds. They appear indifferent to every thing around them; abject, servile, and brutish."

If the native intelligence and buoyant independence of Britons cannot survive in the dank and baleful climate of personal slavery, could it be reasonably expected that the poor Africans, unsupported by any consciousness of personal dignity or civil rights, should not yield to the malignant influences to which they had so long been subjected, and be depressed even below the level of the human species? But at Sierra Leone, they have resumed the stature and port of men, and have acquired, in an eminent degree, the virtues of the citizen and the subject. Witness the peace, and order, and loyalty which have generally prevailed in this colony, in a remarkable degree; especially under the present excellent Governor, Sir Charles McCarthy. Still more, these recent savages, having become the subjects of religious and moral culture, have manifested the greatest willingness to receive instruction, and made a practical proficiency in Christianity, such as might put Europeans to the blush. Not only have they learned with facility the principles of the Christian faith; but they have shewn, by their mutual kindnesses, and by the attachment and gratitude to their worthy pastors and superintendents, that they have derived from their knowledge of Christianity its moral and practical fruits.

The same testimony as to the progress of the Negro children, in common school learning, has been given by all the masters who have instructed them in the Island of Hayti; and the missionaries, in our different West Indian islands, testify, with one consent, the gratitude and attachment which the West Indian, no less than the Sierra Leone Negroes feel to those who condescend to become their teachers.

Again, the impression so assiduously attempted heretofore to be made, that the *indolence* of the Negro race was utterly incurable, and that without the driving whip they never would willingly engage in agricultural labour, has been shewn to be utterly without foundation. Mr. Parke relates, that the Africans, when prompted by any adequate motives, would work diligently and perseveringly both in agricultural and manufacturing labours. And there is on the African coast a whole nation of the most muscular men and the hardiest labourers, who, from their known industry, are hired both for government service, and by the European traders, as workmen, both on ship-board and on shore.

Nor have instances of a similar kind been wanting even in the West Indies, whenever circumstances have been at all favourable to voluntary industry. Since the dissolution of the black corps, (a measure which the abolitionists are scarcely, I fear, excusable for not having opposed, though prompted to acquiesce in it by unwillingness to thwart, when not indispensably necessary, the prejudices of the colonists) many of the disbanded soldiers have maintained themselves by their own agricultural labours, and have manifested a degree of industry that ought to have silenced for ever all imputations on the diligence of their race. But another still more striking instance has been lately afforded in Trinidad. There many hundreds of American Negroes, at the close of the late unhappy war with the United States, were, by the humane policy of Sir Ralph Woodford, received into Trinidad, to the no small alarm of the planters. These were slaves enfranchised by desertion, yet instead of becoming a nuisance to the community by idleness and dissolute manners, as prejudice loudly foretold, they have maintained themselves well, in various ways, by their own industry and prudence. Many of them have worked as hired labourers for the planters with so much diligence and good conduct, that they are now universally regarded as a valuable acquisition to the colony; and it is supposed, that a large addition to their number would be very gladly received.

Are all these important lessons to be read to us without producing any influence on our minds? Ought they not to enforce on us, as by a voice from heaven, that we have been most cruelly and inexcusably degrading, to the level of brutes, those whom the Almighty had made capable of enjoying our own civil blessings in this world, not less clearly than he has fitted them to be heirs of our common immortality?

progress made in it is the best and greatest achievement yet performed by mankind, and it was hardly to be expected at this period of the world that we should be enjoined, by way of a great reform in human affairs, to begin *un*doing it.

The age, it appears, is ill with a most pernicious disease, which infects all its proceedings, and of which the conduct of this country in regard to the Negroes is a prominent symptom— the Disease of Philanthropy. 'Sunk in deep froth-oceans of Benevolence, Fraternity, Emancipation-principle, Christian Philanthropy, and other most amiable-looking, but most baseless, and, in the end, baleful and all-bewildering jargon,' the product of 'hearts left destitute of any earnest guidance, and disbelieving that there ever was any, Christian or heathen,' the 'human species' is 'reduced to believe in rose-pink sentimentalism alone.' On this alleged condition of the human species I shall have something to say presently. But I must first set my anti-philanthropic opponent right on a matter of fact. He entirely misunderstands the great national revolt of the conscience of this country against slavery and the slave-trade, if he supposes it to have been an affair of sentiment. In depended no more on human feelings than any cause which so irresistibly appealed to them must necessarily do. Its first victories were gained while the lash yet ruled uncontested in the barrack-yard and the rod in schools, and while men were still hanged by dozens for stealing to the value of forty shillings. It triumphed because it was the cause of justice; and, in the estimation of the great majority of its supporters, of religion. Its originators and leaders were persons of a stern sense of moral obligation, who, in the spirit of the religion of their time, seldom spoke much of benevolence and philanthropy, but often of duty, crime, and sin. For nearly two centuries had negroes, many thousands annually, been seized by force or treachery and carried off to the West Indies to be worked to death, literally to death; for it was the received maxim, the acknowledged dictate of good economy, to wear them out quickly and import more. In this fact every other possible cruelty, tyranny, and wanton oppression was by implication included. And the motive on the part of the slave-owners was the love of gold; or, to speak more truly, of vulgar and puerile ostentation. I have yet to learn that anything more detestable than this has been done by human beings towards human beings in any part of the earth. It is a mockery to talk of comparing it with Ireland. And this went on, not, like Irish beggary, because England had not the skill to prevent it,—not merely by the sufferance, but by the laws of the English nation. At last, however, there were found men, in growing number, who determined not to rest until the iniquity was extirpated; who made the destruction of it as much the business and end of their lives, as ordinary men make their private interests; who would not be content with softening its hideous features, and making it less intolerable to the sight, but would stop at nothing short of its utter and irrevocable extinction. I am so far from seeing anything contemptible in this resolution, that, in my sober opinion, the persons who formed and executed it deserve to be numbered among those, not numerous in any age, who have led noble lives according to their lights, and laid on mankind a debt of permanent gratitude.

After fifty years of toil and sacrifice, the object was accomplished, and the negroes, freed from the despotism of their fellow-beings, were left to themselves, and to the chances which the arrangements of existing society provide for those who have no resource but their labour. These chances proved favourable to them, and, for the last ten years, they afford the unusual spectacle of a labouring class whose labour bears so high a price that they can exist in comfort on the wages of a comparatively small quantity of work. This, to the ex-slave-owners, is an inconvenience; but I have not yet heard that any of them has been reduced to beg his bread, or even to dig for it, as the negro, however scandalously he enjoys himself, still must: a carriage or some other luxury the less, is in most cases, I believe, the limit of their privations—no very hard measure of retributive justice; those who have had tyrannical power taken away from them, may think themselves fortunate if they come so well off; at all events, it is an embarrassment out of which the nation is not called on to help them: if they cannot continue to realize their large incomes without more labourers, let them find them, and bring them from where they can best be procured, only not by force.

Let me say a few words on this 'gospel of work'—which, to my mind, as justly deserves the name of a cant as any of those which he has opposed, while the truth it contains is immeasurably farther from being the whole truth than that contained in the words Benevolence, Fraternity, or any other of his catalogue of contemptibilities. To give it a rational meaning, it must first be known what he means by work. Does work mean every thing which people *do?* No; or he would not reproach people with doing no work. Does it mean laborious exertion? No; for many a day spent in killing game, includes more muscular fatigue than a day's ploughing. Does it mean *useful* exertion? But your contributor always scoffs at the idea of utility. Does he mean that all persons ought to earn their living? But some earn their living by doing nothing, and some by doing mischief; and the negroes, whom he despises, still do earn by labour the 'pumpkins' they consume and the finery they wear.

Work, I imagine, is not a good in itself. There is nothing laudable in work for work's sake. To work voluntarily for a worthy object is laudable; but what constitutes a worthy object? On this matter, the oracle of which your contributor is the prophet has never yet been prevailed on to declare itself. He revolves in an eternal circle round the idea of work, as if turning up the earth, or driving a shuttle or a quill, were ends in themselves, and the ends of human existence. Yet, even in the case of the most sublime service to humanity, it is not because it is work that it is worthy; the worth lies in the service itself, and in the will to render it—the noble feelings of which it is the fruit; and if the nobleness of will is proved by other evidence than work, as for instance by danger or sacrifice, there is the same worthiness. While we talk only of work, and not of its object, we are far from the root of the matter; or if it may be called the root, it is a root without flower or fruit.

Your contributor's notions of justice and proprietary right are of another kind than these. According to him, the whole West Indies belong to the whites: the negroes have no claim there, to either land or food, but by their sufferance. 'It was not Black Quashee, or those he represents, that made those West India islands what they are.' I submit, that those who furnished the thews and sinews really had something to do with the matter. 'Under the soil of Jamaica the bones of many thousand British men'—'brave Colonel Fortescue, brave Colonel Sedgwick, brave Colonel Brayne,' and divers others, 'had to be laid.' How many hundred thousand African men laid their bones there, after having had their lives pressed out by slow or fierce torture? They could have better done without Colonel Fortescue, than Colonel Fortescue could have done without them. But he was the stronger, and could 'compel;' what they did and suffered therefore goes for nothing. Not only they did not, but it seems they *could* not have cultivated those islands. 'Never by art of his' (the negro) 'could one pumpkin have grown there to solace any human throat.' They grow pumpkins, however, and more than pumpkins, in a very similar country, their native Africa. We are told to look at Haiti: what does your contributor know of Haiti? 'Little or no sugar growing, black Peter exterminating black Paul, and where a garden of the Hesperides might be, nothing but a tropical dog-kennel and pestigerous jungle.' Are we to listen to arguments grounded on hearsays like these? In what is black Haiti worse than white Mexico? If the truth were known, how much worse is it than white Spain?

But the great ethical doctrine of the Discourse, than which a doctrine more damnable, I should think, never was propounded by a professed moral reformer, is, that one kind of human beings are born servants to another kind. 'You will have to be servants,' he tells the negroes, 'to those that are born *wiser* than you, that are born lords of you—servants to the whites, if they are (as what mortal can doubt that they are?) born wiser than you.' I do not hold him to the absurd letter of his dictum; it belongs to the mannerism in which he is enthralled like a child in swaddling clothes. By 'born wiser,' I will suppose him to mean, born more capable of wisdom: a proposition which, he says, no mortal can doubt, but which I will make bold to say, that a full moiety of all thinking persons, who have attended to the subject, either doubt or positively deny. Among the things for which your contributor professes entire disrespect, is the analytical examination of human nature. It is by analytical examination that we have learned whatever we know of the laws of external nature; and if he had not disdained to apply the same mode of investigation to the laws of the formation of character, he would have escaped the vulgar error of imputing every difference which he finds among human beings to an original difference of nature. As well might it be said, that of two trees, sprung from the same stock, one cannot be taller than another but from greater vigour in the original seedling. Is nothing to be attributed to soil, nothing to climate, nothing to difference of exposure—has no storm swept over the one and not the other, no lightning scathed it, no beast browsed on it, no insects preyed on it, no passing stranger stript off its leaves or its bark? If the trees grew near together, may not the one which, by whatever accident, grew up first, have retarded the other's developement by its shade? Human beings are subject to an infinitely greater variety of accidents and external influences than trees, and have infinitely more operation in impairing the growth of one another; since those who begin by being strongest, have almost always hitherto used their strength to keep the others weak. What the original differences are among human beings, I know no more than your contributor, and no less; it is one of the questions not yet satisfactorily answered in the natural history of the species. This, however, is well known—that spontaneous improvement, beyond a very low grade,—improvement by internal developement, without aid from other individuals or peoples—is one of the rarest phenomena in history; and whenever known to have occurred, was the result of an extraordinary combination of advantages; in addition doubtless to many accidents of which all trace is now lost. No argument against the capacity of negroes for improvement, could be drawn from their not being one of these rare exceptions. It is curious withal, that the earliest known civilization was, we have the strongest reason to believe, a negro civilization. The original Egyptians are inferred, from the evidence of their sculptures, to have been a negro race: it was from negroes, therefore, that the Greeks learnt their first lessons in civilization; and to the records and traditions of these negroes did the Greek philosophers to the very end of their career resort (I do not say with much fruit) as a treasury of mysterious wisdom. But I again renounce all advantage from facts: were the whites born ever so superior in intelligence to the blacks, and competent by nature to instruct and advise them, it would not be the less monstrous to assert that they had therefore a right either to subdue them by force, or circumvent them by superior skill; to throw upon them the toils and hardships of life, reserving for themselves, under the mis-applied name of work, its agreeable excitements.

Were I to point out, even in the highest terms, every vul-nerable point in your contributor's Discourse, I should produce a longer dissertation than his. One instance more must suffice. If labour is wanted, it is a very obvious idea to import labourers; and if negroes are best suited to the climate, to import negroes. This is a mode of adjusting the balance between work and labourers, quite in accordance with received principles: it is neither before nor behind the existing moralities of the world: and since it would accomplish the object of making the negroes work more, your contributor at least, it might have been supposed, would have approved of it. On the contrary, this prospect is to him the most dismal of all; for either 'the new Africans, after labouring a little,' will 'take to pumpkins like the others,' or if so many of them come that they will be obliged to work for their living, there will be 'a black Ireland.' The labour market admits of three possible conditions, and not, as this would imply, of only two. Either, first, the labourers can live almost without working, which is said to be the case in Demerara; or, secondly, which is the common case, they can live by working, but must work in order to live; or, thirdly, they cannot by working get a sufficient living, which is the case in Ireland. Your contributor sees only the extreme cases, but no possibility of the medium. If Africans are imported, he thinks there must either be so few of them, that they will not need to work, or so many, that although they work, they will not be able to live.

Let me say a few words on the general quarrel of your contributor with the present age. Every age has its faults, and is indebted to those who point them out. Our own age needs this service as much as others; but it is not to be concluded that it has degenerated from former ages, because its faults are different. We must beware, too, of mistaking its virtues for faults, merely because, as is inevitable, its faults mingle with its virtues and colour them. Your contributor thinks that the age has too much humanity, is too anxious to abolish pain. I affirm on the contrary, that it has too little humanity—is most culpably indifferent to the subject: and I point to any day's police reports as the proof. I am not now accusing the brutal portion of the population, but the humane portion; if they were humane *enough*, they would have contrived long ago to prevent these daily atrocities. It is not by excess of a good quality that the age is in fault, but by deficiency—deficiency even of philanthropy, and still more of other qualities wherewith to balance and direct what philanthropy it has. An 'Universal Abolition of Pain Association' may serve to point a sarcasm, but can any worthier object of endeavour be pointed out than that of diminishing pain? Is the labour which ends in growing spices noble, and not that which lessens the mass of suffering? We are told, with a triumphant air, as if it were a thing to be glad of, that 'the Destinies' proceed in a 'terrible manner;' and this manner will not cease 'for soft sawder or philanthropic stump-oratory;' but whatever the means may be, it *has* ceased in no inconsiderable degree, and is ceasing more and more: every year the 'terrible manner,' in some department or other, is made a little less terrible. Is our cholera comparable to the old pestilence—our hospitals to the old lazar-houses—our workhouses to the hanging of vagrants—our prisons to those visited by Howard? It is precisely *because* we have succeeded in abolishing so much pain, because pain and its infliction are no longer familiar as our daily bread, that we are so much more shocked by what remains of it than our ancestors were, or than in your contributor's opinion we ought to be.

But (however it be with pain in general) the abolition of the infliction of pain by the mere will of a human being, the abolition, in short, of despotism, seems to be, in a peculiar degree, the occupation of this age; and it would be difficult to shew that any age had undertaken a worthier. Though we cannot extirpate all pain, we can, if we are sufficiently determined upon it, abolish all tyranny: one of the greatest victories yet gained over that enemy is slave-emancipation, and all Europe is struggling, with various success, towards further conquests over it. If, in the pursuit of this, we lose sight of any object equally important; if we forget that freedom is not the only thing necessary for human beings, let us be thankful to any one who points out what is wanting; but let us not consent to turn back.

That this country should turn back, in the matter of negro slavery, I have not the smallest apprehension. There is, however, another place where that tyranny still flourishes, but now for the first time finds itself seriously in danger. At this crisis of American slavery, when the decisive conflict between right and iniquity seems about to commence, your contributor steps in, and flings this missile, loaded with the weight of his reputation, into the abolitionist camp. The words of English writers of celebrity are words of power on the other side of the ocean; and the owners of human flesh, who probably thought they had not an honest man on their side between the Atlantic and the Vistula, will welcome such an auxiliary. Circulated as his dissertation will probably be, by those whose interests profit by it, from one end of the American Union to the other, I hardly know of an act by which one person could have done so much mischief as this may possibly do; and I hold that by thus acting, he has made himself an instrument of what an able writer in the *Inquirer* justly calls 'a true work of the devil.'

Notes

Introduction

1. Edward Long, *Candid Reflections* . . . , London, 1772, *46*.
2. P. D. Curtin, *The Slave Trade; A Census*, Wisconsin, 1969; a compendium of American scholarship at its best.
3. Eric Williams, *Capitalism and Slavery*, Chapel Hill, N. Carolina, 1944; R. B. Sheridan, "The Plantation Revolution and the Industrial Revolution, 1625–1775", *Caribbean Studies*, October 1969, vol. 9, no. 3.
4. Quoted in Eric Williams, *From Columbus to Castro: The History of the Caribbean, 1492–1969*, London, 1970, *136*.
5. *Ibid.*, *136–137*.
6. Walter Rodney, *History of the Upper Guinea Coast, 1554–1800*, Oxford, 1970, *102–104*.
7. J. Matthews, *A Voyage to the River Sierra Leone*, London, 1788, *161*.
8. *Gentleman's Magazine*, 1764, *493*.
9. G. Francklyn, *Observations*. . . , London, 1789, *xl*.
10. James Tobin, *A Farewell Address*, London, 1788, *28–29*.
11. *Acts of the Privy Council*, XXVI, 1596–1597, *16*.
12. *Ibid.*, *20*.
13. See chapter 3 below.
14. *Calendar of State Papers, Domestic*, 1595–1597, *381*; 1589–1601, *199*.
15. *Returns of Aliens*, 1598, vol. III, *407*.
16. *Notes and Queries*, 1961, *168*.
17. E. M. Leonard, *The Early History of the English Poor Relief*, Cambridge, 1907, *297n*.
18. *Calendar of State Papers, Domestic*, 1627–1628, *521*; 1667–1668, *59*; K. L. Little, *Negroes in Britain*, London, 1948, *166*.

208

19. *Calendar of State Papers, Domestic*, 1620, *131*; *Journal of Negro History*, 1942, vol. 27, *88*.

20. See the comments of Sir John Fielding, chapter 3 below.

21. D. M. George, *London Life in the Eighteenth Century*, London, 1925, *134–138*.

22. See the comments of Equiano, chapter 3 below; J. J. Hecht, *Continental and Colonial Servants in Eighteenth Century England*, Northampton, Mass., 1954, *48–49*.

23. See chapters 3 and 4 below for Equiano's description of his own and another slave kidnapping.

24. Some indication of the frequency of slave runaways can be gauged by the fact that large numbers of all the newspaper advertisements concerning slaves are for their recovery and not for their sale. A sample of both types of advertisements can be seen in chapter 3 below.

25. This figure has to be treated with caution. While it is impressionistic and can in no way be measured against any acceptable objective assessment, contemporaries were prepared to accept it as reflecting their experience of the black community. See "Somerset's Case" in chapter 3, below; and Edward Long, "Postscript", *op. cit.*, *75–76*, for a different assessment of the numbers.

26. See chapter 4 below.

27. R. Hallett, *The Penetration of Africa*, London, 1965, *148*.

28. *Ibid.*, *147*.

29. For an illustration—in a totally different but illuminating context—of the differing impact of theology and church organisation, see E. P. Thompson's treatment of the relationship between Methodism and the embryonic working class in *The Making of the English Working Class*, London (Pelican Books edition), 1968. See in particular the postscript to this controversial but enormously stimulating book.

30. For the origins of the English settlement of Sierra Leone, see Richard West, *Back to Africa*, London, 1970; P. Hoare, *Memoirs of Granville Sharp*, London, 1820; C. Fyfe, *Sierra Leone Inheritance*, London, 1964; Equiano, *Interesting Narrative of the Life of Olaudah Equiano* . . . , 2 vols., London, 1789, II.

31. The manuscript papers of Granville Sharp make frequent reference to meetings between Sharp and Equiano. See *Diaries and Letter Books, Granville Sharp Papers*, Hardwicke Court.

32. Winthrop Jordan, *White over Black*, Chapel Hill, N. Carolina, 1968, *19*. A masterly work of scholarship which intimidates as it invigorates any would-be researcher in this field.

33. Malcolm Letts, ed., *Sir John Mandeville's Travels*, Hakluyt Society, London, 1953.

34. David Hume, *Essays, Moral, Political and Literary*, eds., T. H. Green and T. H. Grose, 2 vols., London, 1875, I, *252*; quoted in *Gentleman's Magazine*, 1771, *594*.

35. Bryan Edwards, *The History, civil and commercial, of the British Colonies in the West Indies*, 2 vols., London, 1793, II, *82*.

36. Elsa Goveia, *The West India slave laws of the 18th Century*, Caribbean Universities Press, 1970.

37. William Blackstone, *Commentaries on the Laws of England*, Oxford, 1773, I, *127*.

38. *Journal of Negro History*, vol. XVIII, 1933, *417–420*.

39. William Knox, *Three Tracts . . .* , London, 1768, *15*.

40. "Cartwright's Case, 1569" in H. T. Catterall, *Judicial Cases Concerning American Slavery and the Negro*, 5 vols., Washington, 1926, I, *9*.

41. "Butts v. Penny, 1677", *Ibid.*, I, *9*.

42. *Ibid.*, I, *10* note 3.

43. Yorke-Talbot Opinion, 1729, *Ibid.*, I, *12*, quoted in chapter 5 below.

44. Quoted in *A Letter to Philo-Africanus . . .* , London, 1788, *33*.

45. Catterall, *op. cit.*, I, *12–13*.

46. "Shanley v. Harvey, 1762", *Ibid.*, I, *13*.

47. See chapter 5 below; P. Hoare, *Memoirs of Granville Sharp*; Thomas Clarkson, *The History of the Rise, Progress and Accomplishment of the Slave Trade*, 2 vols., London, 1808, I, *77*; J. Nadelhaft, "The Somerset Case and Slavery", *Journal of Negro History*, vol. LI, 1966.

48. *Granville Sharp Papers*, Box 56, Book G, *12*.

49. J. Nadelhaft, *op. cit.*

50. See chapter 5 below.

51. Quoted in *A Letter to Philo Africanus . . .* , *op. cit.*, *39*.

52. J. Nadelhaft, *op. cit.*, *201*.

53. J. J. Hecht, *op. cit.*, *49*.

54. "The Slave Grace, 1827", Catterall, *op. cit.*, I, *34–37*; Equiano, chapter 4 below; John Latimer, *Annals of Bristol in the Eighteenth Century*, Frome, 1893, *492*.

55. "Keane v. Boycott, 1795", Catterall, *op. cit.*, I, *21*.

56. Benjamin Silliman, *A Journal of Travels in England, Holland and Scotland in the Years 1805 and 1806*, New Haven, Conn., 1820, *271–272*.

57. Eric Williams, *History of the Caribbean, op. cit.*, chapter 17.

58. For the philanthropists' campaigns see R. Coupland, *Wilberforce*, Oxford, 1923; R. Coupland, *The Anti-Slavery Movement*, London, 1933; L. J. Ragatz, *The Fall of the Planter Class in the British Caribbean, 1763–1833*, London, 1928; F. J. Klingberg, *The Anti-Slavery Movement in England*, Newhaven, Conn., 1926; W. L. Mathieson, *British Slavery and its Abolition, 1823–1838*, London, 1926.

59. John Wesley, *Thoughts upon Slavery*, London, 1774; extracts in chapter 7 below.

60. James Pope-Hennessy, *Sins of the Fathers*, London, 1967, contains the most recent comments on Clarkson, but the definitive account of Clarkson's role in the abolition movement still remains his own *History . . . of the Abolition of the Slave Trade*.

61. This is not to deny the attention given to the West Indies in, for instance, the controversy over the encumbered estates, or the brutal reminder in the Governor Eyre controversy of Britain's continuing responsibility. These were however the exception rather than the rule and British political attention by the mid-nineteenth century was focussed firmly on other parts of the world.

62. Racial attitudes and thinking continued of course to mature. But from the mid-Victorian years the Negro was no longer the main focus. C. Bolt, *Victorian Attitudes to Race*, London, 1971.

Chapter 1: The Impact of the African on English Thought

1. George Best, "Discourse" in Richard Hakluyt, *The Principal Navigations, Voyages, Traffiques and Discoveries of the English Nation*, 12 vols., Glasgow, 1904, VII, *262–264*.

2. Sir Thomas Browne, "Enquiries into Vulgar and Common Errors", in G. Keynes, ed., *The Works of Sir Thomas Browne*, London, 1964.

3. See in particular chapter 3 below.

Chapter 2: The African trade

1. Elizabeth Donnan, *Documents Illustrative of the Slave Trade to America*, 4 vols., Washington, 1930–1935, I.
2. J. A. Williamson, *Hawkins of Plymouth*, London, 1949. The most detailed account of the Hawkins family history.
3. "The First Voyage of John Hawkins, 1562–1563", Hakluyt, *op. cit.*, X, *7–8*.
4. J. W. Blake, *European Beginnings in West Africa*, New York, 1937, chapters 7 and 8.
5. For a detailed history of the Company see K. G. Davies, *The Royal African Company*, London, 1957.
6. M. Postlewayt, *The National and Private Advantages of the African Trade Considered*, London, 1746, *1–7*.
7. The best collection of sixteenth and seventeenth century tracts arguing the mercantilist versus free trade case can be found in the Goldsmith's Library, University of London.
8. R. Norris, *Memoirs of the Reign of Bossa Ahadee . . .* , London, 1789, *161–175*.

Chapter 3: The Black Presence in England

1. "John Lok's Second Voyage to Guinea, 1554–1555", Hakluyt, *op. cit.*, VI, *176*. This is not to deny the strong possibility that Africans were brought to England before this time, via the Iberian trade. My concern here is with those whose development as a minority group in England was related directly to the growth of English trading ties with West Africa and, later, the New World.
2. "Licensing Casper van Senden to Deport Negroes" (1601?), *Tudor Royal Proclamations*, P. L. Hughes and J. F. Larkin, eds., New Haven, Conn., 1969, III, *221–222*.
3. Samuel Pepys, for instance, employed a black servant girl in the 1660s; quoted in K. L. Little, *op. cit.*, *166*.
4. Eric Williams, *History of the Caribbean*, *op. cit.*, chapter 9.
5. Proclamation of 1731, Guildhall Record Office, London.
6. L. Radzinovicz, *History of English Criminal Law*, 4 vols., London,

1948–1968, IV, *43–78*; a gold-mine of information for the social historian.

7. J. Fielding, *Penal Laws*, London, 1768, *144–145*.
8. Edward Long ("A Planter"), *Candid Reflections upon the judgment lately awarded by the court of the King's bench in Westminster Hall on what is commonly called 'the negro case'*, London, 1772, *46–76*.
9. Olaudah Equiano, *Interesting Narrative of the life of Olaudah Equiano, or Gustavus Vassa, the African, written by himself*, 2 vols., London, 1789, I, *103–179*.

Chapter 4: The free black voice

1. *Letters of the Late Ignatius Sancho*, 2 vols., London, 1784, *95–97*.
2. Ottobah Cugoano, *Thoughts and Sentiments. . .*, London, 1787, *138–139*.
3. Olaudah Equiano, *Interesting Narrative, op. cit.*, I, *46–77*; II, *119–123*.
4. It is interesting to compare Equiano's description of seeing whites for the first time with Hakluyt's accounts of the early English encounters with Africans; see, for instance, the "Voyage of John Lok, 1554", Hakluyt, *op. cit.*, VI.

Chapter 5: Slavery and English Law

1. For the best analysis of English law and slavery see, H. G. Catterall, *Judicial Cases concerning American Slavery and the Negro*, Washington, 1926, I.
2. *A Letter to Philo-Africanus . . .*, London, 1788, *33–34*; also in Catterall, *op. cit.*, I, *12*.
3. "The Case of James Sommersett, 1772", *Howell's State Trials*, XX.
4. Jerome Nadelhaft, "The Somerset Case and Slavery", *op. cit.*
5. See Equiano, chapter 4 above.
6. The first definitive date for slave importations by the Portuguese into the West Indies is 1505. *Cf.*, E. Donnan, *op. cit.*, I, *14*.

Chapter 6: Black Caricature

1. Edward Long, *History of Jamaica*, 3 vols., London, 1774, II, *351–383*.
2. Bryan Edwards, *The History, civil and commercial of the British colonies in the West Indies*, 2 vols., London, 1793, II, *78–89*.
3. Thomas Carlyle, "Discourse on the Nigger Question", first published in *Fraser's Magazine*, December 1849; taken here from his *Critical and Miscellaneous Essays*, London, 1872, VII, *80–109*.
4. Anthony Trollope, *The West Indies and the Spanish Main*, London, 1859, *55–69*.

Chapter 7: The Humanitarian Impulse

1. Granville Sharp, *A Representation of the Injustice and Dangerous Tendancy of Admitting the least claims to Private Property in the Persons of Men in England*, London, 1769, *42–105*.
2. John Wesley, *Thoughts Upon Slavery*, London, 1774.
3. James Ramsay, *An Essay on the Treatment and Conversion of African Slaves in the British Sugar Colonies*, London, 1784, *231–239*.
4. Thomas Clarkson, *An Essay on the Slavery and Commerce of the Human Species*, London, 1786, *164–216*.
5. William Dickson, *Letters on Slavery, London*, 1789, *61–80*.
6. William Wilberforce, *An appeal . . . in behalf of the Negro Slaves in the West Indies*, London, 1823, *passim*.

Bibliography

Manuscript, Primary

Granville Sharp Papers, Hardwicke Court, Gloucester.

Printed, Primary

Calendar of State Papers, Domestic
Acts of the Privy Council.
Howell's State Trials, vol. 20.
Gentleman's Magazine.

Pamphlet Collection

Goldsmith's Library, London, 50 vols.
   Pamphlets on the Slave Trade, 17 vols.
   Tracts on West Indian Slavery, 17 vols.
   Tracts on Slave Trade, 11 vols.
   Tracts of the Anti-Slavery Society, 2 vols.
   Abolition of the Slave Trade, 2 vols.
   Abridgement, Slave Trade, 1 vol.

Documentary Collections

H. T. Catterall, *Judicial Cases Concerning American Slavery and the Negro*, 5 vols., Washington, 1926–1937.
Elizabeth Donnan, *Documents Illustrative of the Slave Trade to America*, 4 vols., Washington, 1930–1935.

Richard Hakluyt, *The Principal Navigations, Traffiques and Discoveries of the English Nation*, 12 vols., Glasgow, 1904.

P. L. Hughes and J. F. Larkin, *Tudor Royal Proclamations*, New Haven, Conn., 1969, vol. 3.

Eric Williams, *Documents of West Indian History, 1492–1655*, Port of Spain, 1963.

Contemporary Printed

William Blackstone, *Commentaries*, Oxford, 1773.

Sir Thomas Browne, "Enquiries into Vulgar and Common Errors", reprinted in G. Keynes, ed., *The Works of Sir Thomas Browne*, 4 vols., London, 1964.

Thomas Carlyle, "Discourse on the Nigger Question", in *Critical and Miscellaneous Essays*, London, 1872, vol. 7.

Thomas Clarkson, *An Essay on the Slavery and Commerce of the Human Species*, London, 1786.

 History of the Rise, Progress and Accomplishment of the Abolition of the Slave Trade, 2 vols., London, 1808.

Ottobah Cugoano, *Thoughts and Sentiments on the Evil and Wicked Traffic of the Human Species*, London, 1787.

William Dickson, *Letters on Slavery*, London, 1789.

Bryan Edwards, *The History, civil and commercial of the British colonies in the West Indies*, 2 vols., London, 1793.

Olaudah Equiano, *Interesting Narrative of the life of Olaudah Equiano, or Gustavus Vassa, the African, written by himself*, 2 vols., London, 1789.

J. Fielding, *Penal Laws*, London, 1768.

G. Francklyn, *Observations . . .* , London, 1789.

P. Hoare, *Memoirs of Granville Sharp*, London, 1820.

Letters of Ignatius Sancho, 2 vols., London, 1784.

William Knox, *Three Tracts . . .* , London, 1768.

M. Letts, ed., *Sir John Mandeville's Travels*, Hakluyt Society, London, 1953.

Edward Long, *Candid Reflections upon the judgment lately awarded by the court of the King's bench in Westminster Hall on what is commonly called 'the negro case'*, London, 1772.

 History of Jamaica, 3 vols., London, 1774.

J. Matthews, *A Voyage to the River Sierra Leone*, London, 1788.

R. Norris, *Memoirs of the Reign of Bossa Ahadee*, London, 1789.

M. Postlewayt, *The National and Private Advantages of the African Trade Considered* . . . , London, 1746.

James Ramsay, *An Essay on the Treatment and Conversion of African Slaves in the British Sugar Colonies*, London, 1784.

Granville Sharp, *A Representation of the Injustice and Dangerous Tendancy of Tolerating Slavery or of Admitting the least claims to Private Property in the Persons of Men in England*, London, 1769.

Benjamin Silliman, *A Journal of Travels in England, Holland and Scotland in the Years 1805 and 1806*, New Haven, Conn., 1820.

James Tobin, *A Farewell Address*, London, 1788.

Anthony Trollope, *The West Indies and the Spanish Main*, London, 1859.

John Wesley, *Thoughts Upon Slavery*, London, 1774.

William Wilberforce, *An Appeal . . . in behalf of the Negro Slaves in the West Indies*, London, 1823.

Anon., *A Letter to Philo-Africanus* . . . , London, 1788.

The History of Mary Prince, London, 1831.

Secondary Works

J. W. Blake, *European Beginnings in West Africa*, New York, 1937.

C. Bolt, *Victorian Attitudes to Race*, London, 1971.

C. R. Boxer, *The Portuguese Seaborne Empire, 1415–1825*, London, 1969.

R. Coupland, *Wilberforce*, Oxford, 1923.

The British Anti-Slavery Movement, London, 1933.

M. J. Craton and J. Walvin, *A Jamaican Plantation*, London and Toronto, 1970.

P. D. Curtin, *The Image of Africa*, Wisconsin, 1964.

Africa Remembered, Wisconsin, 1967.

The Slave Trade: A Census, Wisconsin, 1969.

Basil Davidson, *Black Mother*, London, 1968.

K. G. Davis, *The Royal African Company*, London, 1957.

R. B. Davis, *The Problem of Slavery in Western Culture*, Ithaca, 1968.

C. Fyfe, *History of Sierra Leone*, London, 1962.

Sierra Leone Inheritance, London, 1964.

D. M. George, *London Life in the Eighteenth Century*, London, 1925.

Elsa Goveia, *The West India Slave Laws of the 18th Century*, Caribbean Universities Press, 1970.

R. Hallett, *The Penetration of Africa*, London, 1965.

J. J. Hecht, *Continental and Colonial Servants in eighteenth century England*, Northampton, Mass., 1954.

E. Jones, *Othello's Countrymen*, London, 1965.

Winthrop Jordan, *White over Black*, Chapel Hill, N. Carolina, 1968.

F. J. Klingberg, *The Anti-Slavery Movement in England*, New Haven, Conn., 1926.

J. Latimer, *Annals of Bristol in the Eighteenth Century*, Frome, 1893.

R. B. Le Page, *Jamaica Creole*, London, 1960.

K. L. Little, *Negroes in Britain*, London, 1948.

C. M. MacInnes, *England and Slavery*, Bristol, 1934.

Averil Mackenzie-Grieve, *The Last Years of the English Slave Trade*, Liverpool, 1941.

D. P. Mannix and M. Cowley, *Black Cargoes*, London, 1963.

W. L. Mathieson, *British Slavery and its Abolition, 1823–1838*, London, 1926.

V. S. Naipaul, *The Loss of El Dorado*, London, 1970.

A. P. Newton, *The European Nations in the West Indies, 1492–1688*, London, 1933.

B. Pares, *War and Trade in the West Indies*, Oxford, 1936.
   Merchants and Planters, Cambridge, 1960.

J. H. Parry, *The Age of Reconaissance*, London, 1963.

Orlando Patterson, *The Sociology of Slavery*, London, 1967.

F. W. Pitman, *The Development of the British West Indies*, New Haven, Conn., 1917.

James Pope-Hennessy, *Sins of the Fathers; A Study of the Atlantic Slave Traders*, London, 1967.

L. Radzinovicz, *History of English Criminal Law*, 4 vols., London, 1948–1968.

L. J. Ragatz, *The Fall of the Planter Class in the British Carribbean, 1763–1833*, London, 1928.
   A Guide to the Study of British Caribbean History, Washington, 1930.

Walter Rodney, *History of the Upper Guinea Coast, 1545–1800*, Oxford, 1970.

R. B. Sheridan, *The Development of the Plantations to 1750*, Caribbean Universities Press, 1970.

Richard West, *Back to Africa*, London, 1970.

Eric Williams, *Capitalism and Slavery*, Chapel Hill, N. Carolina, 1944.
   British Historians and the West Indies, London, 1966.
   From Columbus to Castro: The History of the Caribbean, 1492–1969, London, 1970.

J. A. Williamson, *Hawkins of Plymouth*, London, 1949.

Index to Documents

Index

DATE DUE

6/26			
GAYLORD			PRINTED IN U.S.A.